Practical Debugging in Java™

S. L. Bartlett, A. R. Ford, T. J. Teorey
and G. S. Tyson
University of Michigan

PEARSON

Prentice
Hall

Upper Saddle River, NJ 07458

Library of Congress Cataloging-in-Publication Data
Available on file

Vice President and Editorial Director, ECS: *Marcia J. Horton*
Senior Acquisitions Editor: *Petra Recter*
Editorial Assistant: *Michael Giacobbe*
Vice President and Director of Production and Manufacturing, ESM: *David W. Riccardi*
Executive Managing Editor: *Vince O'Brien*
Managing Editor: *Camille Trentacoste*
Production Editor: *Maria C. Massey*
Director of Creative Services: *Paul Belfanti*
Creative Director: *Carole Anson*
Art Director: *Jayne Conte*
Art Editor: *Greg Dulles*
Cover Designer: *Suzanne Behnke*
Cover Photo: *Peter Steyn / Photo Access / Getty Images*
Manufacturing Manager: *Trudy Pisciotti*
Manufacturing Buyer: *Lisa McDowell*
Marketing Manager: *Pamela Shaffer*
Marketing Assistant: *Barrie Reinhold*

© 2004 Pearson Education, Inc.
Pearson Prentice Hall
Pearson Education, Inc.
Upper Saddle River, NJ 07458

The author and publisher of this book have used their best efforts in preparing this book. These efforts include the development, research, and testing of the theories and programs to determine their effectiveness. The author and publisher make no warranty of any kind, expressed or implied, with regard to these programs or the documentation contained in this book. The author and publisher shall not be liable in any event for incidental or consequential damages in connection with, or arising out of, the furnishing, performance, or use of these programs.

Printed in the United States of America

10 9 8 7 6 5 4 3 2 1

ISBN 0-13-142781-4

Pearson Education Ltd., *London*
Pearson Education Australia Pty. Ltd., *Sydney*
Pearson Education Singapore, Pte. Ltd.
Pearson Education North Asia Ltd., *Hong Kong*
Pearson Education Canada, Inc., *Toronto*
Pearson Educacíon de Mexico, S.A. de C.V.
Pearson Education—Japan, *Tokyo*
Pearson Education Malaysia, Pte. Ltd.
Pearson Education, Inc., *Upper Saddle River, New Jersey*

Dedications

*To TJT, without whose gentle and patient prodding,
I never would have finished my part.*

—Sandra Bartlett

To my mother, Jane, who passed a passion for education on to me.

—Ann Ford

To Bessie, who refused to give in to mediocrity and was an inspiration.

—Toby Teorey

*To all those students who read this book before coming
to my office hours.*

—Gary Tyson

Contents

Preface

This book is a tutorial on debugging techniques for both the beginning and intermediate programmer. For the beginning programmer, it is meant to be a companion book to any introduction to programming in Java. The ideal use of the volume is for the student to take it to the computer lab for quick reference when writing and debugging Java programs. For the intermediate programmer, particularly one with some experience in other languages, this guide provides a quick, up-to-speed primer in Java debugging with a series of examples of common syntax and semantic errors and how they can be detected and corrected.

The motivation for the book came as a result of innumerable sessions in the computer lab with introductory programming classes at the University of Michigan. Unfortunately, many beginning programmers subscribe to the "programming by blind faith" method, writing a complete program, then hoping that it will run correctly the first time without their doing any intermediate testing, and then panicking when the program crashes or generates bad data that cannot be explained. Each time they come to us with "What do I do now?" we go back to the program together to look over the basic logic and then start inserting traces to check the intermediate results and localize the sources of error. We have come to the conclusion that students need a short, clear debugging guide as a valuable addition to their programming skills— something they can easily carry with them and that will supplement their textbooks on introductory programming.

Chapter 1 is a short motivational chapter that summarizes the sources of errors in computer programs.

Chapter 2 describes the most common syntactic and semantic programming errors, with illustrative examples, and explains how to correct them.

Chapter 3 shows the student how to use output statements (System.out. println) to trace variables in Java programs and how tracing can easily be inserted into his or her own programs. Several examples are given to illustrate how tracing can help find bugs, especially when a program runs without any runtime errors, but the results are incorrect. Tracing also is useful for finding errors quickly when the program crashes with an error message or just hangs up, leaving the programmer with no option but to kill the program and reboot the computer, over and over, until the bug is found.

Chapter 4 illustrates how to use a debugger effectively as a follow-on to the tracing method set forth in Chapter 3. Most compilers come with debuggers now, and students need to be able to use them at some point during their first course in programming and in all subsequent programming courses or work activities. Differences among the commonly used debuggers—Sun ONE Studio 4, Borland JBuilder 5 Professional, and Microsoft Visual J++—are described in detail. We strongly recommend that students learn to use both tracing and the debugger as alternative approaches.

The appendices give a summary of the most common bugs found in first Java programs and a checklist of techniques for error detection and prevention.

WHO SHOULD READ THIS BOOK?

Beginning programmers will like this book because it is a quick read with many simple examples, both numeric and nonnumeric. The book should save them many frustrating hours of debugging time when they apply the tracing and system debugger techniques illustrated in Chapters 3 and 4. Furthermore, anyone using the book can easily read any chapter independently of the others. This independence should also appeal to more experienced programmers who want to review their knowledge of debugging without having to wade through all the fundamentals. Instructors in introductory programming classes will want to recommend the book to their students because it will enable the students to be much more self-sufficient in debugging, greatly reducing the time they need for individual counseling regarding their programs.

HOW TO USE THE BOOK

Beginning programmers should peruse Chapters 1 and 2 to get an overview of the basic types of errors that programmers make. Chapter 3 has a self-contained discussion of how to use tracing in your programs with a minimum of effort. Chapter 4 can be read later, when you feel that you need more debugging options, especially for larger programs.

ACKNOWLEDGMENTS

The authors thank James Huddleston and Gavin Osborne for their detailed and insightful critiques of this book.

CHAPTER 1

Introduction

1.1 CHAPTER OBJECTIVES

- To motivate the programmer to learn and use debugging skills from the start
- To understand what types of errors occur in programs
- To learn what types of debugging tools and techniques are generally available to find and correct these different types of errors

1.2 MOTIVATION FOR DEBUGGING SKILLS

We all have read numerous stories of the results of poor programming, from banking errors that result in the loss (or gain) of funds for no apparent reason, to medical record mistakes, to spacecraft communication systems that go awry. In some cases, serious injury or worse has been caused by public transportation failures or medical equipment failures due to computer software errors. These spectacular problems have led to the rise in importance of professional ethics and responsibility of the computing profession to try to minimize and eventually remove the sources of errors.

These problems are often the results of errors or "bugs" that were introduced into the software code by the programmer and were never detected or corrected. In order to minimize the errors you get in programs, it is extremely important to learn the skills of good programming early and keep them constantly in mind. An excellent reference for good programming design and implementation is the popular book *The Practice of Programming* by Kernighan and Pike. (See the bibliography.)

The best time to learn debugging methods is when you first learn to program. That is likely the time you will create your first bug. Learning a systematic way to locate program errors will reduce much of the frustration common to first-time programmers. We wouldn't write this book without knowing how to revise the content. It would be too difficult to "get it right" the first time—and programming languages are much less forgiving than readers.

1.3   FINDING AND CORRECTING ERRORS

Good programming skills are learned through hard work and attention to detail. A well-designed program will eliminate many, but not all, errors. Program coding will often generate errors, even for a well-designed system, and the code will need to be closely checked at all stages of implementation. Compilers, which translate your source code into machine-executable code, will check your syntax and generate error messages, so you can quickly find the errors and correct them.

After the syntax errors have been corrected, you are mostly on your own to find so-called semantic (meaning) errors—that is, code which has correct syntax, but still has incorrect logic and thus generates errors during program execution. Some of these errors are very hard to detect, so you need to develop special skills to find them. It is the main purpose of this book to give you the skills necessary to find and correct semantic errors. That can be achieved either through carefully placed Java output statements highlighting the changes in variables at different locations in the program or by understanding the information with the use of an interactive debugger.

Many errors that occur during program execution may be due less to program logic than to data values that cause problems. A typical example of such an error occurs when the denominator becomes zero just before a division operation is attempted and the system throws an ArithmeticException. Another example is a program that expects numeric data and receives words instead. In that case, a NumberFormatException might be thrown. These types of errors can often be detected and corrected with tracing techniques or the use of a debugger. They can also be detected and dealt with automatically in Java by using exception-handling techniques, but this approach is beyond the scope of the book. (For a detailed discussion of exception handling, see Deitel and Deitel, 2003.)

Some errors are created by bad input data and are not necessarily the fault of the programmer. However, it is still the programmer's duty to include in his or her code ways to check for bad input data, to generate error messages when bad data is found, and, in some cases, to terminate program execution. This is often referred to as "error-checking" code.

Finally, errors do not always manifest themselves at the location at which they occur. A bug may incorrectly modify variables that are unused until much later in execution, at a different location in the program. These errors can be difficult to locate, since the effect is not localized to the line containing the erroneous code.

There are four basic steps involved in debugging any program:

1. determining that an error exists,
2. identifying the type of error,
3. locating the error in the code, and
4. correcting the incorrect code.

It is important to emphasize that these steps are most beneficial when performed for each component (roughly each method) during the initial stages of programming, not after the entire program is written. For example, if the program inputs some data, debug the input method(s) before you start manipulating the data; it is common for a student to stare for hours at a program, manipulating incorrect data—it is hard to find the error when you are looking at the wrong code. By systematically testing each component separately, you isolate most errors and save a lot of time.

1.4 APPROACHES TO DEBUGGING

When semantic or other runtime errors occur, there are three basic approaches you can take to try to find what the problem is and how to correct it.

1. Trace by hand

In this approach, you look at a program listing and trace each step of program execution by hand, trying to re-create the results of the actual program execution. This is usually a good starting point for error correction, especially with small programs or simple methods. It forces you to think through the program logic in a methodical manner. With large programs, the process can be very time consuming, and you may then have to resort to computer-aided (program) tracing.

Tracing by hand is often the first, and sometimes only, technique a programmer uses to find errors. Unfortunately, the probability of finding an error drops rapidly after a few minutes; staring at your code for hours is both frustrating and almost universally fruitless. It is a sure sign of a programmer with little skill at debugging.

2. Program tracing

A systematic method of debugging can eliminate, or at least significantly reduce, the frustration many programmers feel when their program doesn't work. Program tracing (see Chapter 3) uses tracing (print) statements inserted into programs at key locations to track the changing values of variables so that you can see how the program is progressing, step by step. Basic tracing can be done by inserting individual System.out.println statements and using them to specify the location of the trace and the current value of all variables. Extended tracing involves the use of flags and method calls to make the tracing easier to turn on and off and to minimize the amount of code that has to be written and inserted into the program.

3. System interactive debugger

Most programming language environments in use today include a debugger (see Chapter 4)—a software package that allows you to run your program in a step-by-step mode, automatically keeping track of all variables in the program as it executes one step (statement) at a time. You can also set breakpoints, allowing the program to run free of tracing overhead up to a certain location, and then stop to display all the program variables and their values.

All of these debugging techniques are valuable to understand and use. We recommend that you start with tracing by hand because it forces you to make sure that you fully understand a program's requirements and what the program logic is doing. When tracing by hand is no longer giving you any insight about where to locate runtime errors, we recommend the extensive use of program tracing with inserted output statements. In most programs, this method will find all semantic and other runtime errors and should be sufficient. In some cases, however, you may want to use the system interactive debugger. The choice between program tracing and using the system debugger is often one of personal style, but it is important to know how to use both, so that your choice is an informed one. Now, on with the details of debugging!

CHAPTER 2

Common Syntax, Runtime, and Semantic Errors

2.1 CHAPTER OBJECTIVES

- To understand the fundamental characteristics of syntax, runtime, and semantic errors
- To be able to identify specific common syntax, runtime, and semantic errors frequently encountered by beginning programmers
- To be able to interpret a syntax warning
- To be able to apply appropriate techniques to correct these common errors

2.2 SYNTAX ERRORS

A *syntax error* is a violation of the syntax, or grammatical rules, of a natural language or a programming language. The following sentence contains an error in English syntax:

```
I is going to the concert tonight.
```

If we write or say this sentence, other English speakers will know that we have used incorrect grammar, but they will still understand what we *mean*. Programming languages are not so forgiving, however: If, for example, we write a line of Java code which contains a syntax error, the compiler does *not* know what we mean. A syntax error is considered a *fatal compilation error*, because the compiler cannot translate a Java program into executable code if even one syntax error is present.

2.2.1 Syntax Errors: Summary of Important Points

- *How are syntax errors detected?* The compiler detects them when you try to compile your program.
- *Why do they occur?* The syntax rules of Java have been violated.
- *Is there object code generated?* No, so you cannot run the program.
- Solution: Find the lines that contain syntax errors, using the compiler's flagged lines and error messages, and then, using your textbook or other Java reference as a guide, correct the errors.
- Remember that, frequently, a syntax error occurs not in the line flagged by your compiler, but in some line *above* that line—often, but not necessarily, the previous line.

2.2.2 Examples: Common Syntax Errors

Some syntax errors are very common, especially for beginning programmers, and the examples that follow should help you identify and correct many syntax errors in whatever program you are currently working on. The syntax diagrams in your Java textbook or a Java reference book should be your ultimate guide in correcting these types of errors.

Different compilers report syntax errors in different formats. For the examples we will examine, we assume that the compiler displays errors in a Java program named "MyProgram.java" in the following way:

```
MyProgram.java:<line number here>: <description of error>
<optional lines with additional error information>
<line where the error occurred>
                <^ marking the location of the error>
```

The first line indicates the file in which the error occurred, points to the line number on which the compiler has identified the error, and then gives a brief description of what the compiler thinks the error is. There may be additional lines giving more information about the error. The next line prints the line from your code. The last line has a caret (^) pointing to the place in the line where the compiler "thinks" the error is.

Compilers that provide a graphical user interface (GUI), using windows and various graphical items to display information for you, may display all such error messages in one window (which we will assume for our discussion here); or they may simply list the program with erroneous lines highlighted or pointed to by an arrow or other graphic, with written error messages shown off to the side. In any event, error messages displayed by different compilers are generally similar.

Here is an important note about compilers: Modern compilers are typically highly accurate in identifying syntax errors and will help you enormously in correcting your code. However, compilers often present two difficult problems for new programmers: (1) They frequently miss reporting an actual error on one line, get "thrown off track," and then report that there are errors on sub-sequent lines that do not have errors. The compiler may then display error messages that are incorrect. (2) After encountering one true syntax error, compilers often generate many incorrect syntax error messages; again, the compiler has been "thrown off track" by a particular error. Why does this occur? Basically, because a compiler is a sophisticated language-processing program and is not impervious to all the possible ways of using (and misusing) a complex language.

What, then, is your best strategy for eliminating syntax errors?

- Display the current list of syntax errors. (Print it if you like.)
- Start at the first error listed, try to correct it, and then recompile your program; typically, many errors will drop out after one error is fixed.
- If you are having trouble with a particular error listed for a specific line, yet you are 100% sure that the line is correct, then search for a syntax error in the lines *above* that line, starting with the line immediately preceding the one under consideration and working backward; usually, though not always, the error will be found in a line that is close to the one flagged.
- Repeat the process until all errors are eliminated.

Specific examples follow.

Missing Semicolon   In the Java code that follows, three declarations are given. Line numbers (chosen arbitrarily in all examples) are shown to the left of each line. Here is the code:

```
5    int number;
6    float value
7    double bigNum;
```

A Java compiler would generate an error something like this:

```
MyProgram.java:6: ';' expected.
float value
           ^
```

To fix this error, just add a semicolon after the identifier value, as in

```
6    float value;
```

Undeclared Variable Name, Version 1   If the preceding code were compiled, and if it included an assignment statement, as in

```
5    int num;
6    float value
7    double bigNum;
8    bigNum = num + value;
```

we would see the following additional error message:

```
MyProgram.java:8: cannot resolve symbol
symbol  : variable bigNum
location: class MyProgram
      bigNum = num + value;
      ^
```

This is a situation in which there is actually no syntax error on the line flagged and the real error occurs on a line above it. Line 8 is, in fact, correct. If we correct the problem in line 6, the error reported for line 8 will drop out the next time we compile the program.

Undeclared Variable Name, Version 2   What about the following code?

```
5    int num;
6    float value;
7    double bigNum;
8    bignum = num + value;
```

We would see the following error message:

```
MyProgram.java:8: cannot resolve symbol
symbol  : variable bignum
location: class MyProgram
      bignum = num + value;
      ^
```

This is a different problem; in this case, an error actually exists on line 8. The lowercase n in `bignum` must be changed to an uppercase N, or else the variable name does not match its declaration. Remember, Java is case sensitive: Lowercase letters are different from uppercase letters.

Undefined Class Name   Consider the following program:

```
1    public class MyProgram extends Applet
2    {
3       public void paint(Graphics g)
4       {
5           g.drawString("Hello World!", 20, 20);
6       }
7    }
```

A compiler will generate an error message like this one:

```
MyProgram.java:1: cannot resolve symbol
symbol  : class Applet
location: class MyProgram
class MyProgram extends Applet
      ^
```

The problem is that `Applet` is defined in a *package* named `java.applet`. To correct this error, we need only add the following line, right before line 1 in the preceding code:

```
import java.applet.Applet;
```

Unmatched Parentheses   Given the code

```
5   result = (firstVal - secondVal / factor;
```

the compiler would generate an error message like

```
MyProgram.java:5: ')' expected
        result = (firstVal - secondVal / factor;
                                              ^
```

Notice that the compiler marks the last possible place you could put the ')' and still have a valid line—right in front of the final semicolon. If you put the ')' where the compiler marked the line, the expression would probably not do what you wanted. To correct the syntax error without introducing a semantic error, we could use the code

```
5   result = (firstVal - secondVal) / factor;
```

Note that similar syntax errors can occur with unmatched braces—{ and }—or with unmatched brackets—[and].

Unterminated String Constants   It is easy to forget the last double quote in a string, as in

```
21    final String ERROR_MESSAGE = "bad data entered!;
```

or

```
45    System.out.println("Execution Terminated);
```

Both commands will provoke the compiler to print something similar to

```
unclosed string literal
```

Both can be fixed by adding the terminating double quote to the string:

```
21    final String ERROR_MESSAGE = "bad data entered!";
```

```
45    System.out.println("Execution Terminated");
```

Left-Hand Side of Assignment Does Not Contain a Variable   Look at the following statements, where the intent of the assignment statement in line 7 is to calculate `x * y` and store the result in `product`:

```
6    double x = 2.0, y = 3.1415, product;
7    x * y = product;
```

The Java compiler will print an error message like this one:

```
MyProgram.java:7: unexpected type
required: variable
found   : value
      x * y = product;
        ^
```

But what does the message mean? A variable is a location in memory where something can be stored. Nothing else is valid in that position. Therefore, we correct the error by using

```
7    product = x * y;
```

Another error that leads to an invalid left-hand side is to forget to include the variable name when you define a variable and initialize it. For example, for the code

```
6    double x = 2.0, y = 3.1415, product;
7    int = 5;
```

the compiler will generate the following error message:

```
MyProgram.java:7: not a statement
    int = 5;
    ^
```

The compiler can't even guess what the code is supposed to do, so it just says that the line isn't a valid statement. It is up to you to figure out what the problem is. In this case, it can be fixed by supplying a variable name in the line to make it a statement:

```
int z = 5;
```

Value-Returning Method Has No Return Statement A method declared with a return type must contain a return statement. Consider the following method, which is supposed to round its float parameter up or down appropriately:

```
10    static int roundFloat (float floatToRound)
11    {
12        int roundedValue;
13        roundedValue = (int) (floatToRound + 0.5);
14    }
```

This method calculates a correct result in the local variable `roundedValue`, but it never returns this result. The compiler will generate the following message:

```
MyProgram.java:11: missing return statement
    {
    ^
```

The message points to the opening brace of the method, so you will easily be able to find the return type and return the proper value. The error can be corrected by adding a return statement, as in

```
10    static int roundFloat (float floatToRound)
11    {
12        int roundedValue;
13        roundedValue = (int) (floatToRound + 0.5);
14        return roundedValue;
15    }
```

Lines of Code Outside of Methods   Class and instance variable declarations can include initialization code, but you are not permitted to have any other executable statements outside a method, a constructor, or an initializer. If your class includes code such as

```
5    class MyProgram
6    {
7        int x;
8        x = 3;
```

the compiler will give you the message

```
MyProgram.java:8: <identifier> expected
    x = 3;
     ^
```

This problem can be corrected with the code

```
5    class MyProgram
6    {
7                int x = 3;
```

or by putting the line of code x = 3; inside the appropriate method body.

Calling a Method with the Wrong Arguments   This common error occurs when the types of the arguments in a method call don't match the types of the parameters in the definition of the method. For example, the random method in the Math class takes no arguments. If you try to call it with an argument, such as

```
8    int randomNumber = Math.random(5);
```

you will get the following error message:

```
MyProgram.java:8: random() in java.lang.Math cannot be
applied to (int)
double randomNumber = Math.random(5);
                      ^
```

Here is another example of mismatched types wherein the compiler gives a different message. If your lines of code look like

```
7    String number = "3";
8    if (number.equals(3))
```

you will get the following error message, since the method is called with an argument, but you have tried to call it with the wrong type of argument:

```
MyProgram.java:8: cannot resolve symbol
symbol   : method equals   (int)
location: class java.lang.String
if (number.equals(3))
           ^
```

In this case, the equals method of the String class must have an Object argument or a String argument—it doesn't work with primitive types. To fix the error, you could do the following:

```
8     if (number.equals("3"))
```

In both of these examples, the error occurs because the types of the arguments in a method call don't match the types of the parameters in the definition of the method. The compiler gives different error messages because, from its point of view, the errors *are* different: The first is using an argument to call a method that doesn't need one, and the second is calling a method with an argument of the wrong type.

Local Variable Not Initialized   If you try to use the value of a local variable (declared inside a method) before you assign a value to the variable, your code will not compile. For example, suppose you have the following variable declarations and code in a method:

```
8     int x, y;
9     y = x * 3;
```

Then the compiler will give the following message:

```
MyProgram.java:9: variable x might not have been
initialized
        y = x * 3;
            ^
```

To correct this error, you must assign a value to x before you use it:

```
8     int x = 7, y;
9     y = x * 3;
```

Using "=" When "==" Is Intended   Given the if statement,

```
20    if (num = 100)
21        System.out.println("num equals 100");
22    else
23        System.out.println("num is not 100");
```

the compiler would display the following error message:

```
MyProgram.java:20: incompatible types
found   : int
```

```
required: boolean
        if (num = 100)
            ^
```

What is the problem with the code? You may have noticed that the equals sign used in the `if` expression is actually an assignment operator, not the relational operator that tests for equality. In this code, num is set to 100 because of the assignment, and the expression num = 100 returns an int, because the value of the expression is actually 100. However, Java conditions must be `boolean`. The corrected code for this example would be

```
20    if (num == 100)
```

2.3 SYNTAX WARNINGS

From the discussion thus far, you know that a syntax error is a *fatal compilation error*; that is, the compiler cannot translate your program into executable code. Compilers also can generate syntax *warning* messages, which do not denote fatal errors and are often helpful in the program development process. Compiler writers, being programmers themselves, are familiar with common programming errors and usually build some error checking of this type into the compiler. Let's look at a few examples.

2.3.1 Syntax Warnings: Summary of Important Points

- *How are nonfatal syntax errors detected?* The compiler detects them when you compile your program.
- *Why do they occur?* The syntax rules of Java have *not* been violated, but the compiler writers have built in special checks for certain common programming errors, and the compiler has found a possible error of this type.
- *Is there object code generated?* Yes, so you can run the program.
- Solution: Find the lines that contain the syntax warnings, and check them very carefully to see if you think they contain genuine errors.
- Remember, a syntax warning should *always* be taken seriously, because there may be a real error in your code if the compiler issues a warning message.

2.3.2 Examples: Common Syntax Warnings

The most common syntax warning you will get from the Java compiler is a *deprecation warning*. This means that you are using an old version of a method which will be removed from the Java language sometime in the future. To get rid of the warning, look in Sun's on-line API documentation to find the new method that replaces it. Here is an example of code that will generate a deprecation warning from the compiler:

```
8    Panel p = new Panel();
9    Dimension d = p.size();
```

When you compile the program that contains these lines, you get this warning:

```
Note:  MyProgram.java uses or overrides a deprecated API.
Note:  Recompile with -deprecation for details.
```

The program has been compiled and you can run it.

To find the lines in your code that are causing the warning, recompile the code with the deprecation flag, as in

```
javac -deprecation MyProgram.java
```

Now the compiler will give you detailed information about which methods are deprecated and where they are used in your code:

```
MyProgram.java:9: warning: size() in java.awt.Component
has been deprecated
    p.size();
     ^
```

If you know the name of the newer version of the method, you can substitute it into your code. If you don't know the name of the newer version, go to the API and look in the Component class for the size() method. There it will tell you that size() has been replaced by getSize(). To eliminate the deprecation warning, replace the old version of the method with the new one:

```
8    Panel p = new Panel();
9    Dimension d = p.getSize();
```

This code will compile without a warning.

2.4 RUNTIME ERRORS

A *runtime error* is an abnormal event that disrupts the normal execution of a program. It is like a pen running out of ink or getting a cream pie in the face in the middle of a sentence:

```
I will be going to
```

The reader or listener is left with an incomplete idea. When a runtime error occurs in a progam, the program immediately stops executing at that point; its computation is incomplete. Some runtime errors are caused by bugs in the code, some are caused by bad input, and some are due to hardware or software problems in the computer itself (e.g., a hard-disk crash or insufficient memory).

2.4.1   Runtime Errors: Summary of Important Points

- *How are runtime errors detected?* Runtime errors are detected by the person using the program.
- *Why do they occur?* The Java Virtual Machine has been asked to do something it can't do.
- *Is there object code generated?* Yes, so you can run the program.
- Solution: Study the error message that is printed, find the values that caused the runtime error, using extra print statements, hand tracing, or an interactive debugger if needed, and correct the errors.
- Remember, runtime errors occur when the program is executed, so be sure to test your programs thoroughly, with different kinds of input.

2.4.2   Examples: Common Runtime Errors

Using Objects That Are Null   If you use an object before you assign it a value, your program will generate a NullPointerException and stop executing. For example, suppose you are building a Graphical User Interface and you want to add a JButton with this code:

```
24    JPanel buttonPanel;
25    public MyProgram()
26    {
27        buttonPanel.add(new JButton("Start"));
```

The code will compile, but when you run it, you will get an error message similar to the following:

```
Exception in thread "main" java.lang.NullPointerException
        at MyProgram.<init>(MyProgram.java:27)
        at MyProgram.main(MyProgram.java:45)
```

Notice that the error message tells you which line in your code caused the NullPointerException. Go to that line, and make sure that each object used there has been given a value. The error can be corrected by giving buttonPanel an object to point to:

```
24    JPanel buttonPanel = new JPanel();
25    public MyProgram()
26    {
27        buttonPanel.add(new JButton("Start"));
```

The line that caused the error was not the one which needed fixing. This is usually the case with null pointer exceptions.

Array Index Out of Bounds   If you access an array with an index that is either less than zero or greater than or equal to the size of the array, the Java Runtime will throw an ArrayIndexOutOfBoundsException, and stop the program's execution. For example, consider the following code, which is intended to initialize all the values in an array:

```
10    int [] squares = new int[100];
11    for (int i = 0; i <= 100; i++)
12        squares[i] = i * i;
```

This code will compile and start to run, but you will get an error message similar to this:

```
Exception in thread "main"
java.lang.ArrayIndexOutOfBoundsException
        at MyProgram.main(MyProgram.java:12)
```

Again, the error message tells you which line in your code caused the exception, but that is probably not the line with the error. The error will be in the code which generates the index that is used in the line where the error occurred. This error can be corrected by changing the first line of the `for` loop:

```
10    int [] squares = new int[100];
11    for (int i = 0; i < 100; i++)
12        squares[i] = i * i;
```

2.5 SEMANTIC ERRORS

A *semantic error* (sometimes called a logic error) is a violation of the rules of *meaning* of a natural language or a programming language. The following English sentence contains a semantic error:

```
My refrigerator just drove a car to Chicago.
```

If we write or say this sentence, other English speakers may begin to wonder about our sanity, but they will nevertheless know that our syntax is perfectly correct! Since a compiler checks only for correct use of syntax, it is not able to evaluate whether we have written code whose *meaning* is correct. Semantic errors are much harder to detect and correct than are syntax errors, and they are also more common than syntax errors.

When there are semantic errors in a Java program, the compiler *does* translate the program into executable code. Most semantic errors do *not* generate compiler warnings. When the program is run, however, it does not work correctly.

2.5.1 Semantic Errors: Summary of Important Points

- *How are semantic errors detected?* Semantic errors are detected by the programmer or user of the program, often while reading output and finding that it is incorrect.
- *Why do they occur?* The syntax rules of Java have been correctly followed, but the meaning of the code is incorrect (e.g., through faulty

algorithms, algorithms not translated into Java correctly, values calculated or input erroneously, or an erroneous flow of control).
- *Is object code generated?* Yes, so you can run the program.
- Solution: Find the lines that contain the semantic errors, using extra print statements, hand tracing, or an interactive debugger if needed, and correct the code.
- Remember, semantic errors are undoubtedly the most serious type of error, and they are the hardest to find and correct, so prevention in the form of good design and defensive programming are often your best tools.

2.5.2 Examples: Common Semantic Errors

Using "=" When "==" Is Intended   In Section 2.2.2, you saw that using the assignment operator instead of the equality operator will cause a syntax error. This happens only if the value is not a Boolean. For example, given the if statement

```
20    if (done = true)
21        System.out.println("the job is done");
22    else
23        System.out.println("the job is not done");
```

the compiler won't display any error message, because the value of the assignment is a boolean, which is what the compiler expects. No matter what value "done" had before the if statement, it will be true when it is tested. This type of error is extremely hard to find.

The error can be corrected by changing the = to ==:

```
20    if (done == true)
21        System.out.println("the job is done");
22    else
23        System.out.println("the job is not done");
```

One way to avoid this problem altogether is to give your booleans meaningful names and just use them in conditions, without testing them. If you write your conditions like

```
20    if (done)
21        System.out.println("the job is done");
22    else
23        System.out.println("the job is not done");
```

you will never make the kind of semantic error discussed here.

Infinite Loop   An infinite loop, which repeats endlessly, is created when a programmer writes a loop in which the expression tested never becomes false.

For example, consider the following code, which is intended to read a lower-case 'y' or 'n' from the user:

```
char response;
System.out.println("Please enter (y)es or (n)o -> ");
response = System.in.read();
while ((response != 'y') || (response != 'n'))
{
        System.out.println("Please enter (y)es or (n)o -> ");
        response = System.in.read();
        System.in.read(); // read and ignore the return
}
```

The expression

```
(response != 'y') || response != 'n')
```

is always true, regardless of what input is entered by the user. If the user enters a 'y,' then the first part of the expression is false, but the second part is true. Thus, the entire expression is true because of the OR operator. Hence, the loop is infinite. The following expression is the corrected version, which merely substitutes AND for OR and is false when the user enters either a 'y' or an 'n,' allowing the program to exit the loop:

```
(response != 'y') && (response != 'n')
```

Misunderstanding of Operator Precedence   Misunderstanding of the operator precedence rules can often lead to expressions that are evaluated incorrectly. Consider the following code, which is intended to calculate the number of miles per gallon achieved by a car:

```
milesPerGallon = endMileage - startMileage / gallonsUsed;
```

Since division has higher precedence than subtraction, the arithmetic expression is evaluated incorrectly. The corrected version is

```
milesPerGallon = (endMileage - startMileage) / gallonsUsed;
```

As part of defensive programming, programmers should make liberal use of parentheses to prevent this kind of error. Still, there are times when extra parentheses are not really necessary. Here are two examples of unneeded parentheses:

```
(x * y) + (3 * z)
```

or

```
(x > 3) && (y > 5)
```

Dangling Else   The "dangling else" is a common and subtle error in the flow of control of a nested `if` statement. Remember, compilers ignore indentation and pair an `else` clause with the closest unmatched `if` clause. The following

code is intended to print out the word "both" if the boolean variables relative and friend are both true and print out "neither" if both are false:

```
if (relative)
    if (friend)
        System.out.println("both");
else
    System.out.println("neither");
```

When this code is run, it prints "both" correctly when both boolean variables
are true. However if both variables are false, the code prints nothing. Further,
when relative is true, but friend is false, the code prints "neither!" There
are many ways to fix or rewrite the code; let's consider one common correction here. The following code forces the compiler to pair the else with the
first if, instead of with the second if, and therefore works correctly:

```
if (relative)
{
    if (friend)
        System.out.println("both");
}
else
    System.out.println("neither");
```

Off-by-One Error   The off-by-one error generally describes a loop that iter-
ates one fewer or one more time than it is supposed to. Consider the following
code, which is intended to read in 50 values from the user and keep a running
total:

```
final int NUM_VALUES = 50;
int someValue,
    total = 0;
for (int i = 1; i < NUM_VALUES; i++)
{
    someValue = Integer.parseInt(JOptionPane.
            showInputDialog("Enter an integer ->"));
    total = total + someValue;
}
```

What happens when this code is executed? The user is prompted 49 (not 50)
times, and 49 (not 50) values are read in and summed. The following small
change in the for loop heading fixes the problem:

```
for (int i = 1; i <= NUM_VALUES; i++)
```

Or, alternatively, we might have

```
for (int i = 0; i < NUM_VALUES; i++)
```

Code That Is inside a Loop, but That Does Not Belong There The following code, adapted from the previous example, is intended to read in a series of 50 numbers entered by the user, calculate the running total, and print out both the final total and the average value of all the numbers:

```
final int NUM_VALUES = 50;
int someValue,
    total = 0,
    average;
for (int i = 1; i <= NUM_VALUES; i++)
{
    someValue = Integer.parseInt(JOptionPane.
            showInputDialog("Enter an integer ->"));
    total = total + someValue;
    average = total / NUM_VALUES;
    System.out.println("Total is: " + total);
    System.out.println("Average is: " + average);
}
```

When this code is executed, it produces a disturbing result! The output is very long, because the total and average are both printed out 50 times. Worse, only the last time they are printed are they correct. What is wrong? The last three lines inside the loop do not belong there; they must be placed outside and after the loop in order for the code to work correctly. Here is the corrected version of the code:

```
for (int i = 1; i <= NUM_VALUES; i++)
{
    someValue = Integer.parseInt(JOptionPane.
            showInputDialog("Enter an integer ->"));
    total = total + someValue;
}
average = total / NUM_VALUES;
System.out.println("Total is: " + total);
System.out.println("Average is: " + average);
```

Not Using a Block when One Is Required The following code, adapted from the previous examples, is intended to read in 50 integers and compute their total:

```
int someValue,
    total = 0;
for (int i = 0; i < NUM_VALUES; i++)
    someValue = Integer.parseInt(JOptionPane.
            showInputDialog("Enter an integer ->"));
    total = total + someValue;
```

The programmer has indented the code to show that both the input statement and the addition are inside the loop. However, the compiler interprets things differently. When executed, the code reads input from the user, but only adds the last value entered to `total`. The following code contains a block and is thus correct:

```
for (int i = 0; i < NUM_VALUES; i++)
{
    someValue = Integer.parseInt(JOptionPane.
            showInputDialog("Enter an integer ->"));
    total = total + someValue;
}
```

A FINAL NOTE

This concludes our discussion of syntax errors and warnings, runtime errors, and semantic errors. While working on your programming assignments on a computer, you may wish to keep this book with you as a helpful guide in determining exactly what the compiler is trying to tell you when you see one of its sometimes obscure error messages. In addition, by studying the examples of all of the common errors described in the chapter, you may be able to prevent many of them from occurring in the first place, as you will have the knowledge and the tools to avoid them altogether.

CHAPTER 3

Tracing Techniques for Debugging

3.1 CHAPTER OBJECTIVES

- To understand the principles of program tracing as an effective debugging tool
- To be able to insert tracing code in your program to find runtime errors
- To quickly identify the location of a runtime error and determine the cause of that error
- To use print tracing of method calls and control statements to better understand the flow of execution of a program
- To use print tracing of variables to better understand the data flow of a program

3.2 BASIC TRACING

Print statements are common in all programs; they are used to specify program output, exceptional events, and program errors. In this chapter, we will show that print tracing in Java can also be an effective tool in finding semantic and runtime errors. In much the same way as spelunkers find their way back to the opening of the cave by laying out a path of rope to trace their path from its very beginning, carefully placed print statements can identify the execution path taken by the program; this path may differ from that expected by the programmer. Such statements can also illustrate important program data throughout the execution of the program: parameter values, loop indices, expression values, etc.

Using extra print statements to trace a program's flow is one of the most important methods for debugging that program. We will look at several simple examples of how tracing is done and how it can be of incredible benefit to you when the computer crashes or hangs up and you don't have any idea where the error occurred. We will also see how tracing works when the program runs to completion without any crash or error message, but the output is incorrect. In both cases, you may or may not have a clue as to where the error is occurring, and, unlike the situation with syntax errors that the compiler catches, you may not have any system messages to help in locating the problem.

Tracing is a method of inserting print statements into your program at key locations to print out (or just display on your screen) the current status (current value) of certain variables in your program so that you can see how the values of those variables are changing during the execution of the program. You can follow the execution step by step, if you wish, by putting in print statements after every line of source code. However, that would be wasteful of time and energy: Your trace can be done better if you first carefully select where to insert the print statements so that their output will provide you with the maximum amount of useful debugging information.

Before we discuss the placement of print statements, let's back up a moment and examine the process of debugging in a systematic manner. There are four steps involved in debugging any program:

1. Determining that an error exists
2. Identifying the type of error
3. Locating the error in the code
4. Correcting the incorrect code

These steps are most beneficial when performed on each component (roughly each method) during the initial stages of programming, without waiting until the entire program is written. It is common for a student to stare for hours at a program with an obscure error; it is hard to find the error when you are looking at the wrong code. By systematically testing each component in isolation, you isolate most errors and save a lot of time.

Let's look at the debugging steps in a little more detail:

Step 1: Determining that an error exists.   This is generally the easiest step in programming assignments, and it is always the hardest step in large, "real-world" programs. Just think about all the programs you have used that "broke" for some reason; clearly, there were errors in the program that were not discovered when it was written. In fact, more hours are generally spent testing a program before it is sold than are spent writing it originally—and even then some errors are missed. However, most first-year programming courses make this step fairly easy by providing a project specification containing input and expected output. If your output doesn't match the expected output, then there is an error in your program. You might also have a more direct indicator that an error occurred if your program "crashes" (aborts abnormally), often with a cryptic error message. Congratulate yourself! You are done with the hardest step and you know that you have an error. Now go identify it, find it, and fix it.

Step 2: Identifying the type of error.   There are many different ways to categorize errors, but for the purpose of debugging a program, it is sufficient to answer two questions: Did the program produce some incorrect output, or did the execution go off track in some way (e.g., produce no output, run forever, or generate an exception)? This classification does not tell you much about what the actual error is, but it does help you determine how to use print tracing to locate the bug. If some particular output value is incorrect, start your search by tracing changes to the variable that created the incorrect output; if, by contrast, the execution followed some unexpected path, start tracing the flow of execution from the earliest location at which you suspect that it went wild (or from the beginning of the program if you have no idea). Generally, debugging involves print tracing of both data values and the flow of execution.

Step 3: Locating the error in the code.   You already know where the bug occurred—somewhere between the beginning of the program and the site where you identified the bug. Now all you need to do is narrow the area to a single line in your program. How you go about doing that depends on the type of bug you have. If it is a bad value, locate each assignment to that variable in the code, and add a print statement after the assignment to display the new value. When you identify the incorrect assignment, examine the expression on the right-hand side of the assignment statement. The error is either in the expression or in one of the variables used in the expression. If it is in the expression, you have narrowed the error to a single expression, so go on to step 4. If the error is a bad value in one of the variables in the expression, continue tracing variables. If you have determined that a variable's value is incorrect after it has been read in one of your input methods, then you have narrowed the problem down to a particular input operation.

If your program ends due to an uncaught exception, the error message will usually tell you exactly which line of your code was involved in causing the exception and will print a stack trace showing which methods called your method and were called by it. Printing the values of the variables that occur on the line in your code referred to in the error message will often pinpoint the problem.

As mentioned earlier, sometimes programs fail without generating bad output values. They may perform some invalid operation (e.g., division by zero) or terminate without producing any output. What is necessary in this case is to completely understand the path the program takes while executing. Fortunately, it can be fairly straightforward to follow even the most complex execution path by adding some well-placed print statements. Print statements at the beginning and end of each method will trace all method calls. Similarly, print statements at each control structure (a `while` loop, an `if` statement, a `switch`, etc.) can trace the execution path within a method. Print tracing of the execution path is even more powerful when augmented with print tracing of data values. Perhaps the best example of this synergy is seen in printing all parameters at the entry to each method. Using the combination of execution path tracing and data tracing, one can locate almost any error quickly, without getting stuck. If print tracing is applied to individual components during the initial coding of the program, errors can be identified and corrected quickly.

Step 4: Correcting the incorrect code.   Once you have identified the location of the error, it may seem trivial to fix the code. This is often the case, but more frequently the error involves a misunderstanding about the operation of a method call to a large class library; fixing the error involves studying the interface specification documents for that class (and others that may be referred to by that method). Fortunately, there exists a wealth of information available to programmers, from numerous textbooks on the Java language to websites throughout the world containing detailed information on various class libraries, complete with examples.

If the error still resists your efforts at correction, it is often useful to put down the program you are having difficulty with and work on a small test program related to the error until you really understand the operation of the class, method, or piece of code you are using.

3.2.1   Example 1: School Is More than Studying

Let's look at some simple examples to illustrate the process of using print tracing to locate errors. At the same time, we will demonstrate some of the most common errors that new Java programmers commit. The first program we will consider examines scores for a sporting event and prints out the winning team and score. The program loads scores for four events in women's gymnastics—vault, uneven bars, balance beam, and floor exercise—and then calculates the total score, determines the winning team, and prints the name of the winning team along with its score. Note that some blank lines have been deliberately left in the code to leave room for adding print tracing statements later:

```
1:     import java.io.*;
2:     import java.util.*;
3:
4:     public class GymnasticsWinner
       {
5:
6:         public static void main( String args[] )
                           throws IOException
           {
7:
```

```
8:
9:          double vault, floor, beam, bars, score, topscore;
10:         String inputLine, school, winner = "default";
11:         StringTokenizer tokens;
12:
13:         BufferedReader in = new
                    BufferedReader(newFileReader("testfile"));
14:            topscore = 0;
15:
16:         while ((inputLine = in.readLine()) != null)
               {
17:
18:            tokens = new StringTokenizer(inputLine);
19:            school = tokens.nextToken();
20:
21:            vault = Double.parseDouble(tokens.nextToken());
22:            floor = Double.parseDouble(tokens.nextToken());
23:            beam = Double.parseDouble(tokens.nextToken());
24:            bars = Double.parseDouble(tokens.nextToken());
25:            score = vault + floor + beam + bars;
26:
27:
28:            if (score > topscore)
               {
29:               topscore = score;
30:               winner = school;
31:            }
32:            }
33:            System.out.print ("The winner is " + winner );
34:            System.out.println(" with a score of " + topscore);
35:      } // end public static void main()
36:
37:   } // end class GymnasticsWinner
```

To run this example, we use the scores from the 2002 NCAA Women's Gymnastics Championship. The text file contains lines with a team name, followed by the team score for each of four events. There is a <**tab**> character between the team name and scores and a tab between the scores for each event. The test input file is as follows:

Utah	49.175 49.300 49.350 49.125
Georgia	49.250 49.325 49.375 49.300
California - Los Angeles	49.325 49.375 49.150 49.300
Alabama	49.325 49.450 49.375 49.425
Nebraska	49.075 49.425 48.750 49.175
Stanford	49.075 48.925 49.000 49.025

When this program is executed, an exception is generated, terminating the program before the winning team can be identified. (Well, at least we have completed Step 1 and know that we have an error.) The error message returned was

```
Exception in thread "main" java.lang.NumberFormatException:
For input string: "-" at java.lang.NumberFormatException.forIn-
putString(NumberFormatException.java:48) at java.lang.Floating-
Decimal.readJavaFormatString(FloatingDecimal.java:1213) at
GymnasticsWinner.main (GymnasticsWinner.java:21)
```

It is pretty easy to narrow down where the error manifests itself: somewhere in the parseDouble method called on line **21**. However, that doesn't necessarily tell us where the actual error is. At this point, it might be useful to find out more about the NumberFormatException class. To do so, we look at the java.lang class definition; Sun has the complete API documentation on the Web at

http://java.sun.com/j2se/1.4/docs/api/index.html.

There you will find the following description of the exception type:

```
public class NumberFormatException: Thrown to indicate that the
application has attempted to convert a string to one of the numeric
types, but that the string does not have the appropriate format.
```

This definition suggests that the parameter (the string returned from token.nextToken) does not contain a sequence of digits (0–9) that can be converted into an integer; in fact, the error message tells us that the string which could not be converted was "-". Since the character "-" occurs in only one location in the input ("California - Los Angeles"), it is likely that the error occurred when this line was parsed. We can verify that assumption by adding some print statements in the while loop (lines **16–32**) to track the processing of the input file. In the following code, we show the debug statements in bold.

```
1:    import java.io.*;
2:    import java.util.*;
3:
4:    public class GymnasticsWinner
      {
5:
6:        public static void main( String args[] )
                            throws IOException
          {
7:
8:            final boolean DEBUG = true;
9:            double vault, floor, beam, bars, score, topscore;
```

```
10:          String inputLine, school, winner = "default";
11:          StringTokenizer tokens;
12:
13:              BufferedReader in = new BufferedReader(new
                                    FileReader("testfile"));
14:          topscore = 0;
15:
16:          while ((inputLine = in.readLine()) != null)
             {
17:              if (DEBUG){System.err.println("inputLine:" +
                                                inputLine );;}
18:              tokens = new StringTokenizer(inputLine);
19:              school = tokens.nextToken();
20:              if (DEBUG) { System.out.println("The
                                school is: " + school ); }
21:              vault = Double.parseDouble(tokens.nextToken());
22:              floor = Double.parseDouble(tokens.nextToken());
23:              beam = Double.parseDouble(tokens.nextToken());
24:              bars = Double.parseDouble(tokens.nextToken());
25:              score = vault + floor + beam + bars;
26:              if (DEBUG) { System.out.println("The
                                score is: " + score ); }
27:
28:              if (score > topscore)
                 {
29:                  topscore = score;
30:                  winner = school;
31:              }
32:          }
33:          System.out.print ("The winner is " + winner );
34:          System.out.println(" with a score of " + topscore);
35:      } // end public static void main()
36:
37:      } // end class GymnasticsWinner
```

The first thing to notice in this version of our program is a definition of
DEBUG on line **8**. All later occurrences of **DEBUG** will be replaced with the
constant boolean value **true**. This value will be used to control whether print
tracing is performed throughout the program and will enable us to leave the
debug code in the program after we have completed debugging. Next, we add
a print statement in line **17** to echo each input line read from the file. The print
statement is also placed in an `if` statement so that the debug definition can
control whether printing occurs. (Remember that the value of **DEBUG** is
true.) The same approach is used to print out the school name in line **20** and to
print out the score in line **26**.

Now, when we reexecute the program, it will still fail on a Number-FormatException, but before failing, it will produce the following output to System.err:

```
inputLine: Utah                   49.175 49.300 49.350 49.125
The school is: Utah
The score is:  196.95
inputLine: Georgia                49.250 49.325 49.375 49.300
The school is: Georgia
The score is: 197.25
inputLine: California - Los Angeles   49.325 49.375 49.150 49.300
The school is: California

Exception in thread "main" java.lang.NumberFormatException: For
input string: "-" at java.lang.NumberFormatException.forInput-
String(NumberFormatException.java:48) at java.lang.FloatingDeci-
mal.readJavaFormatString(FloatingDecimal.java:1213) at
GymnasticsWinner.main(Gymnastics Winner.java:21)
```

This output clearly shows the error in parsing team names containing more than one word. The error did not show up in the first two team names (Utah and Georgia), but did when the "California - Los Angeles" team scores were parsed. "California" was placed in the school variable, and the string "-" was used as the vault score. When we passed "-" to parseDouble(), that method could not translate into a double and therefore threw an exception (Number-FormatException). It is now easy to identify the error: nextToken() in line **19** should return the entire school name, delimited by a <tab> character. Now we need to figure out how to fix the code so that the assignment of school name in line **19** (and therefore the calculation of vault score in line **21**) is correct for "California - Los Angeles."

To fix this code, we need to examine the StringTokenizer class in more detail. (See http://java.sun.com/j2se/1.4/docs/api/index.html.) The StringTokenizer class scans a string and returns a series of substrings (or tokens) by means of the nextToken() method. By default, tokens are delimited by spaces, tabs, or newlines. This default is causing the problem, because the input specification says that the team name and scores are delimited by the tab only. The documentation says that we can override the default delimiters in the StringToken() constructor or in the nextToken() method. Since all fields use only tabs as delimiters, we chose to specify the tab delimiter (specified as "\t" in Java) as an argument to the StringToken() constructor shown in line **18** in the final version of the program:

```
1:    import java.io.*;
2:    import java.util.*;
3:
4:    public class GymnasticsWinner
      {
5:
```

```
 6:     public static void main( String args[] )
                            throws IOException
         {
 7:
 8:        final boolean DEBUG = false;
 9:        double vault,floor, beam, bars, score, topscore;
10:        String inputLine, school, winner = "default";
11:        StringTokenizer tokens;
12:
13:        BufferedReader in = new BufferedReader(new
                            FileReader("testfile"));
14:        topscore = 0;
15:
16:        while ((inputLine = in.readLine()) != null)
           {
17:            if (DEBUG) { System.err.println("inputLine:"
                                    + inputLine); }
18:            tokens=new StringTokenizer(inputLine,"\t");
19:            school=tokens.nextToken();
20:            if (DEBUG) { System.out.println("The school is: "
                                    + school ); }
21:            vault = Double.parseDouble(tokens.nextToken());
22:            floor = Double.parseDouble(tokens.nextToken());
23:            beam = Double.parseDouble(tokens.nextToken());
24:            bars = Double.parseDouble(tokens.nextToken());
25:            score = vault + floor + beam + bars;
26:            if (DEBUG) { System.out.println("The score is: "
                                    + score ); }
27:
28:            if (score > topscore)
               {
29:                topscore = score;
30:                winner = school;
31:            }
32:        }
33:        System.out.print ("The winner is " + winner );
34:        System.out.println(" with a score of " + topscore);
35:    } // end public static void main()
36:
37: } // end class  GymnasticsWinner
```

Let's take a closer look at this final version. We have modified a few lines in addition to fixing line 18. Debug printing at lines **17**, **20**, and **26** was retained, but the printing is now suppressed by changing the value of **DEBUG** to **false** in line **8**. When we reexecute the final version of the program, we get the correct output:

```
The winner is Alabama with a score of   197.575
```

There is a lot to digest in this example. We showed how to use print statements to trace both the flow of execution (which iteration of the loop failed) and the flow of data (how "California - Los Angeles" was incorrectly parsed by next-Token()). We showed how to use the declaration of a boolean variable (**DEBUG**) along with `if` statements to control whether debug printing occurs. We applied this debugging technique to one of the most common programming errors: incorrectly reading or parsing some input data. Finally, we had to learn more about the Java language itself by looking at several reference documents during the debug process: NumberFormatException, StringTokenizer, and nextToken. As an exercise, think about how you might debug the program if the input data came directly from the 2002 NCAA Women's Gymnastics Web page. How would the program find that page? How many network class definitions would you need to understand to get to that page? How would you parse the text on that page to extract the scores? How many things could go wrong?

3.2.2   Example 2: Traveling to Lose (or Gain) Weight!

The next example illustrates how a misunderstanding of a control statement can lead to incorrect output and, more importantly, how that type of bug can be systematically found and corrected. This program asks a person's weight and travel plans and then determines the person's new weight at his or her destination (another planet in our solar system). The input consists of a person's earth weight and the destination planet. (We ignore a large number of physical properties that make the travel—or living—impractical.) For simplicity, and to show another form of program input, the person's weight and planet number will be specified as command-line arguments to the program. The original (incorrect) program is as follows:

```
1:     import java.io.*;
2:
3:
4:     public class TravelWeight
       {
5:
6:       public static void main( String args[] )
                            throws IOException
         {
7:         double newWeight;
8:         if (args.length != 2)
           {
```

```
9:            System.err.println("Usage: example2 <weight>
                                      <planet(0-9)>");
10:          System.exit(0);
11:       }
12:
13:    newWeight = calculateWeight(Double.parseDouble(args[0]),
                                Integer.parseInt(args[1]));
14:    System.out.println("Your new weight is: " + newWeight );
15:       }
16:
17:    public static double calculateWeight ( double earthLBS,
                                                int planet )
          {
18:          double newLBS;
19:
20:
21:          switch (planet)
             {
22:             case 1: newLBS = earthLBS * .08;
23:
24:
25:             case 2: newLBS = earthLBS * .89;
26:
27:
28:             case 3: newLBS = earthLBS * 1.0;
29:
30:
31:             case 4: newLBS = earthLBS * .38;
32:
33:
34:             case 5: newLBS = earthLBS * 2.8;
35:
36:
37:             case 6: newLBS = earthLBS * .98;
38:
39:
40:             case 7: newLBS = earthLBS * 1.2;
41:
42:
43:             case 8: newLBS = earthLBS * .78;
44:
45:
46:             case 9: newLBS = earthLBS * .07;
47:
48:
```

```
49:                    default:newLBS = earthLBS * 0.0;
50:
51:
52:              }
53:           return newLBS;
54:       } // end public static double calculateWeight()
55:
56:   } // end class TravelWeight
```

You might see the error right now; it is a very common mistake. However, regardless of whether you see the error, it is the process of debugging this type of error that you should be learning. When you run the preceding program with a weight of 125 and planet number 3 (you are staying on Earth), you should calculate a new weight of 125. Unfortunately, when the program is executed, it prints

Your new weight is: 0

This is a "bad output data" error, but what is the cause? Using the systematic approach to print tracing, we should print out each change to the variable being output, such as **newWeight** in the main() method. As we saw in the first example, print tracing can also be useful in printing out the input values to make sure that we are not performing the new weight calculation on bad input values. The modified version of the program is as follows:

```
1:      import java.io.*;
2:
3:
4:      public class TravelWeight
        {
5:          static final boolean DEBUG = true;
6:          public static void main( String args[] )
                            throws IOException
        {
7:            double newWeight;
8:            if (args.length != 2)
              {
9:                System.err.println("Usage: example2 <weight>
                                           <planet(0-9)>");
10:               System.exit(0);
11:           }
12:           if (DEBUG) {System.err.println("weight: "
                        + args[0] + "; planet: " + args[1]);}
13:           newWeight = calculateWeight(Double.parseDouble(args[0]),
                                      Integer.parseInt(args[1]));
14:           System.out.println("Your new weight is: " + newWeight );
15:       }
```

```
16:
17:       public static double calculateWeight ( double earthLBS,
                                                        int planet )
          {
18:         double newLBS;
19:
20:
21:         switch (planet)
            {
22:            case 1: newLBS = earthLBS * .08;
23:
24:
25:            case 2: newLBS = earthLBS * .89;
26:
27:
28:            case 3: newLBS = earthLBS * 1.0;
29:
30:
31:            case 4: newLBS = earthLBS * .38;
32:
33:
34:            case 5: newLBS = earthLBS * 2.8;
35:
36:
37:            case 6: newLBS = earthLBS * .98;
38:
39:
40:            case 7: newLBS = earthLBS * 1.2;
41:
42:
43:            case 8: newLBS = earthLBS * .78;
44:
45:
46:            case 9: newLBS = earthLBS * .07;
47:
48:
49:            default:newLBS = earthLBS * 0.0;
50:
51:
52:            }
53:         return newLBS;
54:      } // end public static double calculateWeight()
55:
56:    } // end class  TravelWeight
```

Executing this modified program outputs the following debug messages to System.err:

```
weight: 125; planet: 3
```

So we are correctly reading the arguments, but the result is still incorrect. Since newWeight is assigned the value returned by calculateWeight(), we must continue debugging in calculateWeight(). To do this, we add print statements to display changes to the variable newLBS, since it is used to return the method value. These changes are as follows:

```
1:    import java.io.*;
2:
3:
4:    public class TravelWeight
      {
5:        static final boolean DEBUG = true;
6:        public static void main( String args[] )
                           throws IOException
          {
7:          double newWeight;
8:          if (args.length != 2)
            {
9:              System.err.println("Usage: example2 <weight>
                                    <planet(0-9)>");
10:             System.exit(0);
11:         }
12:         if (DEBUG) {System.err.println("weight: "
                    + args[0] + "; planet: " + args[1]);}
13:         newWeight = calculateWeight(Double.parseDouble(args[0]),
                                    Integer.parseInt(args[1]));
14:         System.out.println("Your new weight is: " + newWeight );
15:       }
16:
17:       public static double calculateWeight ( double earthLBS,
                                    int planet )
          {
18:           double newLBS;
19:
20:
21:           switch (planet)
              {
22:             case 1: newLBS = earthLBS * .08;
23:                 if (DEBUG){System.err.println("newLBS:"+
                             String.valueOf(newLBS));}
```

```
24:
25:           case 2: newLBS = earthLBS * .89;
26:               if (DEBUG){System.err.println("newLBS:"+
                                 String.valueOf(newLBS));}
27:
28:           case 3: newLBS = earthLBS * 1.0;
29:               if (DEBUG){System.err.println("newLBS:"+
                                 String.valueOf(newLBS));}
30:
31:           case 4: newLBS = earthLBS * .38;
32:               if (DEBUG){System.err.println("newLBS:"+
                                 String.valueOf(newLBS));}
33:
34:           case 5: newLBS = earthLBS * 2.8;
35:               if (DEBUG){System.err.println("newLBS:"+
                                 String.valueOf(newLBS));}
36:
37:           case 6: newLBS = earthLBS * .98;
38:               if (DEBUG){System.err.println("newLBS:"+
                                 String.valueOf(newLBS));}
39:
40:           case 7: newLBS = earthLBS * 1.2;
41:               if (DEBUG){System.err.println("newLBS:"+
                                 String.valueOf(newLBS));}
42:
43:           case 8: newLBS = earthLBS * .78;
44:               if (DEBUG){System.err.println("newLBS:"+
                                 String.valueOf(newLBS));}
45:
46:           case 9: newLBS = earthLBS * .07;
47:               if (DEBUG){System.err.println("newLBS:"+
                                 String.valueOf(newLBS));}
48:
49:           default:newLBS = earthLBS * 0.0;
50:               if (DEBUG){System.err.println("newLBS:"+
                                 String.valueOf(newLBS));}
51:
52:           }
53:           return newLBS;
54:       } // end public static double calculateWeight()
55:
56: } // end class  TravelWeight
```

When this version of the program is executed, the following text is sent to System.err:

```
EarthWeight: 125; planetNumber 3
EarthLBS: 125; planet: 3
Case 3:newLBS: 125
Case 4:newLBS: 47.125
Case 5:newLBS: 295.5
Case 6:newLBS: 114.5
Case 7:newLBS: 111.125
Case 8:newLBS: 140.625
Case 9:newLBS: 8.375
Default:newLBS: 0
NewWeight: 0
```

Our print tracing shows the error in the flow of execution of this program. The switch statement branched to the correct case, but continued execution through all subsequent cases, including the default, which sets the **newLBS** variable to zero. To correct the code, break statements should be added to each case block. This is one of the most common errors that new programmers commit—so common that it is useful to include print trace code whenever one uses switch statements (at least for the default case). The correct, final version is as follows, with the **DEBUG** variable set to false to suppress the print statements used in debugging:

```
1:     import java.io.*;
2:
3:
4:     public class TravelWeight
       {
5:         static final boolean DEBUG = false;
6:         public static void main( String args[] )
                             throws IOException
           {
7:           double newWeight;
8:           if (args.length != 2)
             {
9:               System.err.println("Usage: example2 <weight>
                                        <planet(0-9)>");
10:              System.exit(0);
11:          }
12:          if (DEBUG) {System.err.println("weight: "
                   + args[0] + "; planet: " + args[1]);}
13:          newWeight = calculateWeight(Double.parseDouble(args[0]),
                                     Integer.parseInt(args[1]));
14:          System.out.println("Your new weight is: " + newWeight );
15:      }
16:
```

```
17:         public static double calculateWeight ( double earthLBS,
                                                   int planet )
            {
18:            double newLBS;
19:
20:
21:            switch (planet)
               {
22:               case 1: newLBS = earthLBS * .08;
23:                   if (DEBUG){System.err.println("newLBS:"+
                               String.valueOf(newLBS));}
24:                  break;
25:               case 2: newLBS = earthLBS * .89;
26:                   if (DEBUG){System.err.println("newLBS:"+
                               String.valueOf(newLBS));}
27:                  break;
28:               case 3: newLBS = earthLBS * 1.0;
29:                   if (DEBUG){System.err.println("newLBS:"+
                               String.valueOf(newLBS));}
30:                  break;
31:               case 4: newLBS = earthLBS * .38;
32:                   if (DEBUG){System.err.println("newLBS:"+
                               String.valueOf(newLBS));}
33:                  break;
34:               case 5: newLBS = earthLBS * 2.8;
35:                   if (DEBUG){System.err.println("newLBS:"+
                               String.valueOf(newLBS));}
36:                  break;
37:               case 6: newLBS = earthLBS * .98;
38:                   if (DEBUG){System.err.println("newLBS:"+
                               String.valueOf(newLBS));}
39:                  break;
40:               case 7: newLBS = earthLBS * 1.2;
41:                   if (DEBUG){System.err.println("newLBS:"+
                               String.valueOf(newLBS));}
42:                  break;
43:               case 8: newLBS = earthLBS * .78;
44:                   if (DEBUG){System.err.println("newLBS:"+
                               String.valueOf(newLBS));}
45:                  break;
46:               case 9: newLBS = earthLBS * .07;
47:                   if (DEBUG){System.err.println("newLBS:"+
                               String.valueOf(newLBS));}
48:                  break;
```

```
49:              default:newLBS = earthLBS * 0.0;
50:                if (DEBUG){System.err.println("newLBS:"+
                                String.valueOf(newLBS));}
51:                break;
52:        }
53:        return newLBS;
54:    } // end public static double calculateWeight()
55:
56:    } // end class  TravelWeight
```

When the final version of this program is executed with arguments 125 and 3, the following, correct output is written to System.out:

```
Your new weight is: 125
```

3.2.3   Example 3: Stock Trading

The final example in this section illustrates some of the difficulties that arise in using print tracing without careful thought. The program automates trading decisions for a simplified stock-trading environment. The goal of the program is to find good heuristics for trading stock. For the purposes of this example, we have greatly simplified the trading patterns simply by using a random-number generator to determine whether certain stock traded up or down each day, so it will be impossible to find a heuristic that trades better than random. However, as an example, we will use a simple trading strategy that calculates an expected value and compares it with the current value to see whether we should buy (or sell) a single share of stock. Trading ends when the program has either doubled the original $1000 cash or halved it. Here is the first attempt at the program:

```
1:     import java.io.*;
2:     import java.util.*;
3:
4:     public class StockTrading
       {
5:
6:        static double cash = 1000.00, stockPrice = 10.0,
                                        expectedPrice;
7:        static int stockShares;
8:
9:        public static void main( String argv[] )
                            throws IOException
          {
10:
11:
```

```
12:
13:        Random marketChange = new Random();
14:
15:        boolean keepTrading = true;
16:
17:        while (keepTrading)
           {
18:
19:
20:          stockPrice = stockPrice
                    + marketChange.nextGaussian();
21:          if (stockPrice <=0) {stockPrice = 0.02;}
22:          expectedPrice = stockPrice
                    + marketChange.nextGaussian();
23:          if (cash > stockPrice && expectedPrice
                                > stockPrice*1.02)
             {
24:              cash = cash - stockPrice;
25:              stockShares = stockShares + 1;
26:
27:          }
28:          if (stockShares > 0 && expectedPrice*1.02
                                    < stockPrice)
             {
29:
30:              cash = cash + stockPrice;
31:              stockShares = stockShares - 1;
32:          }
33:          if (cash+stockShares*stockPrice == 500)
                                { keepTrading = false;}
34:          if (cash+stockShares*stockPrice == 2000)
                                { keepTrading = false;}
35:
36:      }
37:      System.out.println("You now have $"+
                (cash+stockShares*stockPrice));
38:
39:  } // end public static void main()
40:
41:
42:
43:
44:
45:
46:
```

```
47:
48:
49:
50:
51:    } // end class StockTrading
```

If you run this program, you might think that it would print out a cash value of under $500 or over $2000 (certainly, nothing in between). It is theoretically possible that the program will not complete in any given amount of time if you continually trade in the range from $500 to $2000; however, that is extraordinarily unlikely over more than a second or two, since that is sufficient time to make millions of trades. However, if you run the program in its current form, it is almost certain that it will not complete in a second or two (or, for that matter, in the time it takes to read this book). While it is running, let us consider how to debug the program by using the debugging approach in this section.

Step 1: Determine that an error exists.   Well, the program has not terminated in "a reasonable amount of time," so it is likely that there is an error. The statistical nature of this particular program makes it impossible to prove that there is an error; however, time is better spent assuming that there is an error and trying to identify it than waiting for the program to complete, assuming that no error exists and the program is just running an extraordinarily long time.

Step 2: Identifying the type of error.   The program has not produced incorrect output—in fact, it has not produced *any* output or even completed execution. So we should first start by understanding the flow of execution of the program.

Step 3: Locating the error in the code.   We can use print tracing for this purpose, but there are some danger signs, the most important of which is that the program has been running for several minutes and it is possible to execute billions, or even trillions, of print statements in that period. Inserting a bunch of print statements and reexecuting the program is likely to generate an infinite stream of output to System.err (hopefully, to your screen and not redirected to a printer!). There are a couple of ways to deal with this problem: We can limit the frequency of printing, or we can add a new termination condition to end the program much sooner than it is currently ending.

In this particular program, the primary execution path is through the loop starting at line **17** and continuing to line **36**. We could put a print statement at the beginning of the loop, but we expect the loop to iterate millions of times each second. It is more useful to iterate for only the first five times, to see if the stock, trading, and cash values are computed correctly. This approach will reduce the information sent to the screen to a great extent. We can clean up the debug output further by writing a new method that prints all the information that is helpful to debugging the program, including program variables and some expressions (like the total value of stock and cash). The following code shows our first attempt at print tracing:

```
1:    import java.io.*;
2:    import java.util.*;
3:
4:    public class StockTrading
      {
5:
6:        static double cash = 1000.00, stockPrice = 10.0,
                                    expectedPrice;
7:        static int stockShares;
8:
9:        public static void main( String argv[] )
                              throws IOException
          {
10:
11:           final boolean DEBUG = true;
12:           int DEBUG_counter = 0;
13:           Random marketChange = new Random();
14:
15:           boolean keepTrading=true;
16:
17:           while (keepTrading)
              {
18:             if (DEBUG) { DEBUG_counter ++; }
19:             if (DEBUG) { DEBUG_print(DEBUG_counter); }
20:             stockPrice=stockPrice
                      + marketChange.nextGaussian();
21:             if (stockPrice <=0) {stockPrice=0.02;}
22:             expectedPrice = stockPrice
                          + marketChange.nextGaussian();
23:             if (cash > stockPrice && expectedPrice
                                  > stockPrice*1.02)
                {
24:               cash = cash - stockPrice;
25:               stockShares = stockShares + 1;
26:               if (DEBUG) { DEBUG_print("buy" ); }
27:             }
28:             if (stockShares > 0 && expectedPrice*1.02
                                    < stockPrice)
                {
29:               if (DEBUG) { DEBUG_print("sell" ); }
30:               cash = cash + stockPrice;
31:               stockShares = stockShares - 1;
```

```
32:          }
33:          if (cash+stockShares*stockPrice == 500)
                                    { keepTrading = false; }
34:          if (cash+stockShares*stockPrice == 2000)
                                    { keepTrading = false; }
35:          if (DEBUG && DEBUG_counter == 5)
                          {keepTrading = false; }
36:       }
37:       System.out.println("You now have $"+
             (cash+stockShares*stockPrice));

38:
39:   } // end public static void main()
40:
41:   private static void DEBUG_print(String msg )
      {
42:
43:       System.err.println("[" + msg + "]" +
44:           ": cash = " + cash +
45:           ": stockShares = " + stockShares +
46:           ": stockPrice = " + stockPrice +
47:           ": value = "
                    + ( cash+stockShares*stockPrice));
48:
49:   } // end private static void DEBUG_print()
50:
51:   } // end class StockTrading
```

As in the previous examples, we declare **DEBUG** (line **11**) to control the printing of debugging output. In addition, we declare another debug variable (**DEBUG_counter**) to enable early termination of the program. This variable is initialized to zero (line **12**), incremented each iteration through the loop (line **18**), and used to terminate the loop after five iterations (line **35**). This strategy will ensure that the loop, and therefore the program, terminates. (Remember, at this time, we are only trying to determine whether the algorithm is updating the variables correctly.) We also choose to add print statements at three locations in the loop: at the start of each iteration (line **19**), after a share of stock is purchased (line **26**), and when a share of stock is sold (line **29**). At each of these locations, it is useful to print out a variety of data values, as well as the total stock plus cash value used to terminate the program. As in any program, instead of duplicating code throughout the program, it is better coding style to write a method that can be called from each site. We declare the new method **DEBUG_print** at lines **41** through **49**. This method prints the values of the variables **cash**, **stockShares**, and **stockPrice**, as well as the expression (**cash + stockShares × stockPrice**). The method also prints a string argument that is used to identify the location of the call to **DEBUG_print**, and it can provide additional information relevant to that location. The first call to **DEBUG_print** (line **19**) passes a string representation of the loop iteration counter stored in the variable **DEBUG_counter**. The second call to **DEBUG_print** (line **26**) passes the string "**buy**" to indicate that this debug output was generated when a share of stock was purchased. Similarly, the third call to **DEBUG_print** (line **29**) passes the string "**sell**" to indicate that the program is selling a share of stock. When the modified program is executed, the following output is produced to System.err (note that, due to the random nature of the calculation of **stockPrice** and **expectedPrice**, different output is likely on each run):

```
1:    cash = 1000.00: stockShares = 0: stockPrice = 10.00: value = 1000.00
2:    cash = 1000.00: stockShares = 0: stockPrice = 10.23: value = 1000.00
buy:  cash = 988.20:  stockShares = 1: stockPrice = 11.80: value = 1000.00
3:    cash = 988.20:  stockShares = 1: stockPrice = 10.30: value = 998.50
4:    cash = 988.20:  stockShares = 1: stockPrice = 12.50: value = 1000.70
buy:  cash = 976.10:  stockShares = 2: stockPrice = 12.10: value = 1000.30
5:    cash = 976.10:  stockShares = 2: stockPrice = 10.50: value = 997.10
sell: cash = 989.10:  stockShares = 1: stockPrice = 13.00: value = 1002.10
```

This output shows five cycles of trading with two shares purchased and one share sold. It appears that buying and selling stock operate correctly and that the calculation of the total value is correct. We have not yet identified the error, but we have tested a significant portion of the program. Unfortunately, the error doesn't appear during the first few iterations of the loop, so we need to continue execution beyond five iterations. This can easily be achieved by changing the constant 5 in line **35** to a much larger value (say, 5000), but doing so will generate a large number of output lines that must be examined. Accordingly, we will instead use a new technique to reduce the total debug output generated: Limit the frequency of printing by printing out only debugging values every 1000 iterations. This aim can be achieved in a number of ways, the easiest of which is to add a single line to **DEBUG_print()** instructing it to print only if **DEBUG_counter** is a multiple of 1000. This modification is shown in the following code:

```
1:    import java.io.*;
2:    import java.util.*;
3:
4:    public class StockTrading
      {
5:
6:        static double cash = 1000.00, stockPrice = 10.0,
                                        expectedPrice;
7:        static int stockShares;
8:
9:        public static void main( String argv[] )
                            throws IOException
          {
```

```
10:
11:          final boolean DEBUG = true;
12:          int DEBUG_counter = 0;
13:          Random marketChange = new Random();
14:
15:          boolean keepTrading = true;
16:
17:          while (keepTrading)
             {
18:            if (DEBUG) { DEBUG_counter ++; }
19:            if (DEBUG) { DEBUG_print( DEBUG_counter); }
20:            stockPrice = stockPrice
                        + marketChange.nextGaussian();
21:            if (stockPrice <=0) {stockPrice = 0.02;}
22:            expectedPrice = stockPrice
                        + marketChange.nextGaussian();
23:            if (cash > stockPrice && expectedPrice
                                   > stockPrice*1.02)
               {
24:               cash = cash - stockPrice;
25:               stockShares = stockShares + 1;
26:               if (DEBUG) { DEBUG_print("buy" ); }
27:            }
28:            if (stockShares > 0 && expectedPrice*1.02
                                   < stockPrice)
               {
29:               if (DEBUG) { DEBUG_print("sell" ); }
30:               cash = cash + stockPrice;
31:               stockShares = stockShares - 1;
32:            }
33:            if (cash+stockShares*stockPrice == 500)
                                   { keepTrading = false;}
34:            if (cash+stockShares*stockPrice == 2000)
                                   { keepTrading = false;}
35:            if (DEBUG && DEBUG_counter == 5000)
                                   {keepTrading = false; }
36:          }
37:          System.out.println("You now have $"+
                     (cash+stockShares*stockPrice));
38:
39:       } // end public static void main()
40:
41:       private static void DEBUG_print(String msg )
             {
```

```
42:          if (DEBUG_counter % 1000 == 0)
43:            System.err.println("[" + msg + "]" +
44:                "": cash = " + cash +
45:                "": stockShares = " + stockShares +
46:                "": stockPrice = " + stockPrice +
47:                "": value = "
                        + ( cash+stockShares*stockPrice));
48:
49:        } // end private static void DEBUG_print()
50:
51:   } // end class StockTrading
```

The first change made in this version of the program modifies the expression on line **35**, changing 5 to 5000 to allow more iterations of the loop before the program terminates. The second change inserts an `if` statement in line **42** that restricts the printing of debug information to only those iterations which are multiples of 1000 (i.e., at iterations 1000, 2000, 3000, etc.). When this version of the program is executed, the following output is generated:

```
1000: cash = 804.00:   stockShares = 11:   stockPrice = 6.02:   value = 870.22
2000: cash = 436.20:   stockShares = 35:   stockPrice = 12.23:  value = 864.25
3000: cash = 500.82:   stockShares = 68:   stockPrice = 24.31:  value = 2153.90
4000: cash = 1150.13:  stockShares = 33:   stockPrice = 8.50:   value = 1430.63
sell: cash = 1159.23:  stockShares = 32:   stockPrice = 9.10:   value = 1450.43
5000: cash = 820.10:   stockShares = 40:   stockPrice = 15.50:  value = 1440.01
```

When we reexecute the program printing every thousandth iteration, it becomes apparent that the error involves the exit condition of the loop, because the total value exceeded the $2000 limit at iteration 3000 (**value = 2153.90**). This isolates the error to line **34**.

Step 4: Correcting the incorrect code. At this point, the error is easy to detect and simple to fix. The expression in line **34**,

```
(cash + stockShares*stockPrice == 2000)
```

fails to account for the extremely likely case that the value may exceed $2000 instead of being exactly $2000. To fix the error, simply change the **equal to** operator (==) to the **greater than or equal to** operator (>=). Go ahead and make that change, but stop and think about how it will affect the program as a whole. You should also change the expression on line **33** to make sure that you terminate the program if the value drops below $500. What would happen if you changed only the expression in line **34**? How would you debug that program, and which step would be the most difficult to complete?

Here is the final version of our program, with the expressions on lines **33** and **34** corrected and the variable **DEBUG** set to false (on line 11) to suppress debugging output:

```
1:     import java.io.*;
2:     import java.util.*;
3:
4:     public class StockTrading
       {
5:
6:         static double cash = 1000.00, stockPrice = 10.0,
                                              expectedPrice;
7:         static int stockShares;
8:
9:         public static void main( String argv[] )
                           throws IOException
           {
10:
11:          final boolean DEBUG = false;
12:          int DEBUG_counter = 0;
13:          Random marketChange = new Random();
14:
15:          boolean keepTrading = true;
16:
17:          while (keepTrading)
             {
18:             if (DEBUG) { DEBUG_counter ++; }
19:             if (DEBUG) { DEBUG_print( DEBUG_counter); }
20:             stockPrice = stockPrice
                       + marketChange.nextGaussian();
21:             if (stockPrice <=0) {stockPrice = 0.02;}
22:             expectedPrice = stockPrice
                       + marketChange.nextGaussian();
23:             if (cash > stockPrice && expectedPrice
                                   > stockPrice*1.02)
                {
24:                cash = cash - stockPrice;
25:                stockShares = stockShares + 1;
26:                if (DEBUG) { DEBUG_print("buy" ); }
27:             }
28:             if (stockShares > 0 && expectedPrice*1.02
                                   < stockPrice)
                {
29:                if (DEBUG) { DEBUG_print("sell" ); }
30:                cash = cash + stockPrice;
31:                stockShares = stockShares - 1;
32:             }
33:             if (cash+stockShares*stockPrice <= 500)
                                { keepTrading =false; }
```

```
34:                     if (cash+stockShares*stockPrice >= 2000)
                               { keepTrading = false; }
35:               if (DEBUG && DEBUG_counter == 5000)
                          {keepTrading = false; }
36:        }
37:        System.out.println("You now have $"+
               (cash+stockShares*stockPrice));
38:
39:        } // end public static void main()
40:
41:        private static void DEBUG_print(String msg )
           {
42:            if (DEBUG_counter % 1000 == 0)
43:                System.err.println("[" + msg + "]" +
44:                ": cash = " + cash +
45:                ": stockShares = " + stockShares +
46:                ": stockPrice = " + stockPrice +
47:                ": value = "
                        + ( cash+stockShares*stockPrice));
48:
49:        } // end private static void DEBUG_print()
50:
51:    } // end class StockTrading
```

When this final version of the program is executed, it will terminate when the value of stock and cash either exceeds $2000 or falls below $500 and the program prints the amount. For instance, when we ran the corrected program, it completed with the following output sent to System.out:

```
You now have $489.78
```

3.3   USING EXCEPTIONS AND ASSERTIONS TO AID IN FINDING OR AVOIDING ERRORS

While the purpose of the chapter has been to show how print statements can be used to identify and correct errors in an existing program, it is often more efficient to place some debugging information into code as it is being created. In this section, we will examine two proactive measures aimed at reducing common program errors: exception handling of parameters, and assertions.

3.3.1   Exception Handling for Parameter Checking

The Java language includes an extensive exception-handling mechanism to improve program management of error conditions. If you have written even relatively small Java programs, you are probably familiar with some exceptions. One of the more powerful management capabilities is the verification of parameter value ranges for method calls. If we can identify invalid parameters when a method is called, the error is less likely to appear inside the method and will therefore be easier to trace to the bad method call. This is best illustrated by revisiting the calculateWeight() method in Example 2, TravelWeight. What would happen if the method was called with the planet argument asking for the weight on the 10th planet? or the 5th planet? These values are invalid, since it is meaningless to indicate planets that do not exist. It is better to identify the error directly (as an invalid argument to calculateWeight()) than simply to report a default weight of zero. The IllegalArgumentException class is designed to manage this event. In the following code, we add parameter checking to calculateWeight():

```
1:    import java.io.*;
2:    import java.util.*;
3:
4:    public class TravelWeight
      {
5:        static final boolean DEBUG = false;
6:        public static void main( String args[] )
                              throws IOException
          {
7:          double newWeight;
8:          if (args.length != 2)
            {
9:              System.err.println("Usage: example2 <weight>
                                    <planet(0-9)>");
10:             System.exit(0);
11:         }
12:         if (DEBUG) {System.err.println("weight: " + args[0]
                                + "; planet: " + args[1]);}
13:         newWeight = calculateWeight(Double.parseDouble(args[0]),
                                Integer.parseInt(args[1]));
14:         System.out.println("Your new weight is: " + newWeight );
15:       }
16:
17:       public static double calculateWeight ( double earthLBS,
                                        int planet )
          {
18:       double newLBS;
19:       if (planet < 0 || planet > 9)
20:           throw new IllegalArgumentException("Illegal
              planet #" + planet);
21:        switch (planet)
           {
22:            case 1: newLBS = earthLBS * .08;
```

```
23:                    if (DEBUG){System.err.println("newLBS:"+ (newLBS));}
24:                    break;
25:                case 2: newLBS = earthLBS * .89;
26:                    if (DEBUG){System.err.println("newLBS:"+ (newLBS));}
27:                    break;
28:                case 3: newLBS = earthLBS * 1.0;
29:                    if (DEBUG){System.err.println("newLBS:"+ (newLBS));}
30:                    break;
31:                case 4: newLBS = earthLBS * .38;
32:                    if (DEBUG){System.err.println("newLBS:"+ (newLBS));}
33:                    break;
34:                case 5: newLBS = earthLBS * 2.8;
35:                    if (DEBUG){System.err.println("newLBS:"+ (newLBS));}
36:                    break;
37:                case 6: newLBS = earthLBS * .98;
38:                    if (DEBUG){System.err.println("newLBS:"+ (newLBS));}
39:                    break;
40:                case 7: newLBS = earthLBS * 1.2;
41:                    if (DEBUG){System.err.println("newLBS:"+ (newLBS));}
42:                    break;
43:                case 8: newLBS = earthLBS * .78;
44:                    if (DEBUG){System.err.println("newLBS:"+ (newLBS));}
45:                    break;
46:                case 9: newLBS = earthLBS * .07;
47:                    if (DEBUG){System.err.println("newLBS:"+ (newLBS));}
48:                    break;
49:                default:newLBS = earthLBS * 0.0;
50:                    if (DEBUG){System.err.println("newLBS:"+ (newLBS));}
51:                    break;
52:            }
53:        return newLBS;
54:    } // end public static double calculateWeight()
55:
56:    } // end class TravelWeight
```

When you run this version of TravelWeight, asking for your weight on the 10th planet, you get the following error message:

```
Exception in thread "main" java.lang.IllegalArgumentException:
Illegal Planet #10
    at example2.calculateWeight(example2.java:20)
    at example2.main(example2.java:14)
```

This message is much easier to debug than if the program ran without an error being detected and returned the weight as zero. Is there any other parameter checking that should be performed? For very large programs, parameter checking is essential: Without it, an error may manifest itself anywhere in the program. In the unlikely event that we discover a new planet, this exception will identify the need to change the function. Again, the exception will make it easier to track the error (or outdated code) than returning the default weight of zero would. The mechanism isn't foolproof however: If astronomers decide that Pluto is not worthy of being labeled a planet (a question that arises occasionally), then the exception condition will fail to identify the change in specification (namely, that there would then be only eight planets). Still, using exceptions to verify parameter bounds is one of the most important preventative measures a programmer can take when writing code. It localizes the detection of errors, greatly simplifying the location of the erroneous code.

3.3.2   Assertion Checking

The Java language release version 1.4 includes extensions for placing assertions into program code. Assertions provide a powerful mechanism for testing assumptions made in the program without degrading program execution time. An **assert** statement has been added in two forms. The first is

```
assert expression;
```

where expression is a boolean expression. When the assertion is executed, it evaluates the expression and, if it is false, throws an **AssertionError** exception with no detailed message. The second form is

```
assert expression1 : expression2;
```

This version enables you to provide further information when the assertion fails. Expression2 is evaluated and printed when the assertion given in expression1 fails. Expression2 generally returns a String specifying the reason for the assertion failure. To show how assertions can be added to code, we will extend the stock-trading example (StockTrading) to include checks to make sure that we do not iterate the loop when the total value of our assets either exceeds $2000 or falls below $500. If either assertion fails, then the program must be incorrect, since these are the two exit conditions of the loop. The code is as follows:

```
1:     import java.io.*;
2:     import java.util.*;
3:
4:     public class StockTrading
       {
5:
6:         static double cash = 1000.00, stockPrice = 10.0,
                                          expectedPrice;
7:         static int stockShares;
8:
```

```
 9:        public static void main( String argv[] )
                               throws IOException
          {
10:
11:       final boolean DEBUG = false;
12:       int DEBUG_counter=0;
13:       Random marketChange = new Random();
14:
15:        boolean keepTrading = true;
16:
17:        while (keepTrading)
          {
17a:          assert (cash+stockShares*stockPrice < 2000) :
                                         "value too high";
17b:          assert (cash+stockShares*stockPrice > 500) :
                                         "value too low";
18:           if (DEBUG) { DEBUG_counter = DEBUG_counter + 1; }
19:           if (DEBUG) { DEBUG_print( DEBUG_counter); }
20:           stockPrice = stockPrice
                    + marketChange.nextGaussian();
21:           if (stockPrice <=0) {stockPrice = 0.02;}
22:           expectedPrice = stockPrice
                    + marketChange.nextGaussian();
23:           if (cash > stockPrice && expectedPrice
                                    > stockPrice*1.02)
              {
24:              cash = cash - stockPrice;
25:              stockShares = stockShares + 1;
26:              if (DEBUG) { DEBUG_print("buy" ); }
27:           }
28:           if (stockShares > 0 && expectedPrice*1.02
                                    < stockPrice)
              {
29:              if (DEBUG) { DEBUG_print("sell" ); }
30:              cash = cash + stockPrice;
31:              stockShares = stockShares - 1;
32:           }
33:           if (cash+stockShares*stockPrice <= 500)
                              { keepTrading = false;}
34:           if (cash+stockShares*stockPrice >= 2000)
                              { keepTrading = false;}
35:           if (DEBUG && DEBUG_counter == 5000)
                              {keepTrading = false; }
36:       }
```

```
37:                System.out.println("You now have $"+
                       (cash+stockShares*stockPrice));
38:
39:        } // end public static void main()
40:
41:        private static void DEBUG_print(String msg )
           {
42:          if (DEBUG_counter % 1000 == 0)
43:           System.err.println("[" + msg + "]" +
44:                  ": cash = " + cash +
45:                  ": stockShares = " + stockShares +
46:                  ": stockPrice = " + stockPrice +
47:                  ": value = "
                        + ( cash+stockShares*stockPrice));
48:
49:        } // end private static void DEBUG_print()
50:
51:   } // end class StockTrading
```

We added two assertions to this code, at lines **17a** and **17b**. They calculate the total value of assets and check whether the value is in the range from \$500 to \$2000. If either assertions fails, an **AssertionError** exception will occur, printing one of the following error messages:

```
Exception in thread "main" java.lang.AssertionError: value too
high
Exception in thread "main" java.lang.AssertionError: value too
low
```

(*Note*: Depending on the compiler and runtime system used, you may need to set flags to use assertions (e.g., javac ^source 1.4 <source>; java ^ea <java>).

C H A P T E R   4

Using an Interactive Debugger

4.1   CHAPTER OBJECTIVES

- To be able to identify the fundamental commands and tools provided in modern interactive debuggers
- To be able to apply the interactive tools to the debugging and testing of a simple Java program
- To carefully study an example of an interactive debugging task using the Sun ONE Studio 4, Community Edition
- To recognize differences among commonly used interactive Java debuggers, including Borland JBuilder 5 Professional and Microsoft Visual J++ 6.0

4.2   FUNDAMENTALS

In Chapter 3, you learned how to find and correct program bugs by tracing your program's behavior with the use of extra printing statements. In this chapter, you will learn to use an additional tool: the *interactive debugger*. Note that these two tools can be used either separately or together in your work. They share the fundamental goals of pinpointing the locations where program errors occur and discovering what the errors are, while, of course, helping you correct those errors.

An interactive debugger allows you to examine the behavior of your Java program while it is running. A debugger can be an invaluable aid in correcting errors in your code. This chapter describes common tools available in typical modern interactive debugging systems.

The essential idea behind interactive debugging is to discover *critical points* in your program where errors occur. To do this, an interactive debugger lets you stop the program's execution at various points and look at the values of *critical variables* at those points. While the run is suspended, you get a *snapshot* of your program's activity. Execution can then be resumed at the point at which the program run was stopped. In addition, you may observe the program's execution in order to check its *flow of control*, in much the same way as we did with program tracing.

When you check the values of *critical variables*—those you believe to be important in causing your program's problems—the debugger will tell you what values the variables *actually* hold. (*Note*: This may not be the same as what you *want* them to hold or what you *think* they *should* hold.) If the value of some variable is not what you expected, search for the reasons that the value is incorrect. Was it read improperly, calculated improperly, not passed back from a method correctly, or something else?

The *flow of control* in a program is the order in which the program's statements are executed. You can observe this flow by running the program under the control of the debugger, which is capable of executing one statement at a time or many of statements all at once. At all times, the debugger displays a pointer to the statement that is to be executed next. Is the flow of control what you think it should be? Look for dangling elses, missing or out-of-order method calls, infinite loops, and other errors.

We recommend that you refer to Appendix B.3 for a checklist that can help you identify critical variables and important locations in your program's flow of control.

In a typical modern integrated development environment (IDE), you will find that the language compiler is one part of the system and the interactive debugger is another part. To debug your program with the interactive debugger, you must specifically *run* the debugger, which is itself a program. Then, you can run the Java program you are working on by choosing the appropriate command from within the debugging program's menus. In this situation, you are running your Java program under the control of the interactive debugger. Hence, the debugger allows you to observe the behavior of your Java program as it runs.

In this discussion, we will assume that your debugger provides a typical graphical user interface (GUI), using windows and various graphical items to display information for you. Note that if you are using a text-based debugger (such as Sun's command-line debugger jdb), you will still find that the debugging commands and tasks described in this chapter and illustrated with examples using graphics-based debuggers are applicable to your work with a text-based debugger. This is because all debuggers, graphics or text based, provide essentially the same capabilities.

In Sections 4.3 through 4.5, we will study the use of interactive debugging techniques to debug a small sample program. General debugging tools are discussed throughout the chapter. In Sections 4.3 and 4.4, we will specifically study the use of the Sun ONE Studio 4, Community Edition, interactive debugger. If you are using another debugger, it still may be helpful to you to read these sections, as all modern IDEs are similar.

4.3   DEBUGGING WITH SUN ONE STUDIO

4.3.1   Initiating the Debugging Process

The first step in the debugging process is usually to run or activate the interactive debugger by choosing the appropriate menu item in your IDE. The second step involves actually initiating your Java program's execution, under the control of the debugger. In Sun ONE Studio, the debugger is activated automatically when you start a debugging session. Graphics-based IDEs display your program and the debugging information you need in one or more windows on your screen. After you have started debugging your Java program, three new windows typically appear.

One window, called the *Source Editor,* will display the Java program and, if the program is running, will include an arrow that points to the next statement to be executed, which we will call the *current statement indicator.* The *Debugger Window* lets you choose what program information you want to see. Commonly used debug information includes the variables, the call stack, your breakpoints, and your watches. You can also monitor multiple debug sessions and multiple threads or explore any of the classes used in your program. In Sun ONE Studio, you select which types of information to monitor by clicking on the toggle buttons in the toolbar at the top of the Debugger Window. There is also an *Output Window* that lets you see the output of your program as it executes and lets you type in any required input. Figure 4.1 shows Sun ONE Studio's main debugging window.

In the list of variables, you will see the names of variables you have declared, and as the Java program actually runs, you will see the current values of those variables displayed. A variable that has no current value is not displayed in the Variables window. The variables you will see are *local, instance*, and *class* variables that are in the scope of the currently executing method. In Sun ONE Studio, the variables are shown in the Variables window near the bottom of the Debugger Window.

In addition, most systems show a list of the currently active methods by displaying the *call stack*—a list of method calls ordered by when the calls occurred. In Sun ONE Studio, this information is displayed in the Call Stack window near the top of the Debugger Window. It tells you the class in which the method is defined, the name of the method, and the line in the file at which point the method is currently executing. For example, if, during a run, the main method of a class named DoWork called processValues, and processValues called method readOneItem, you would see this list in the Call Stack window:

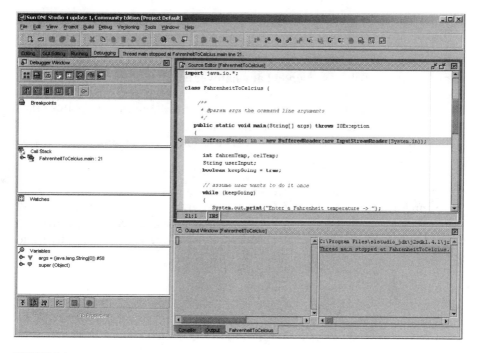

FIGURE 4.1

Sun ONE Studio's main debugging window.

```
DoWork.readOneItem : 249
DoWork.processValues : 123
DoWork.main : 30
```

The currently executing method is at the top of the stack and has a green arrow over its icon. This view of the call stack is also often called a *stack trace*.

4.3.2 Running Your Java Program under Control of the Debugger

After you have activated the debugger and indicated that it must now run your program, the Java program is stored in memory and is ready to execute under the debugger's supervision. The debugger is called *interactive* because you, the programmer, can at any time tell the debugger to display certain values or alter the flow of control of the program. Commands that alter the flow of control include the following:

Start   The **Start** command will start execution of the Java program, at the first statement in the `main` method. If there are no breakpoints set in the program, execution will continue until the program either finishes or crashes. (Breakpoints will be discussed in Section 4.3.4.)

In Sun ONE Studio, you choose **Start** from the **Debug** menu to start the Java program executing.

Pause The **Pause** command can be used to suspend execution of the program. Execution will be suspended at whatever code was executing at the time you choose **Pause**. The program will then stop running, but you can restart it from where it left off, if you like, by choosing **Continue** or any of the other debug commands that allow execution of the code.

In Sun ONE Studio, you choose **Pause** under the **Debug** menu to suspend execution of the program.

Run to Cursor **Run to Cursor** lets you click on the line in the source code in the Source Editor at which you want the program to stop. The program will start executing from its current line and continue until it reaches the line you clicked on. This lets you skip over code that you believe to be error free and get right to the problematic part of your program, where it will pause and let you examine the values of variables, etc.

In Sun ONE Studio, **Run to Cursor** is found in the **Debug** menu.

Finish The **Finish** command halts execution of your Java program.

In Sun ONE Studio, **Finish** is found in the **Debug** menu.

Step Commands A **Step** command allows you to execute one statement: the one pointed at by the current statement indicator. After this single statement is executed, program execution will be suspended again, and you may look at variables or enter another debugging command. Using **Step**, you can observe the effect that one statement has on your program's behavior. Among the various **Step** commands are the following:

Step Over Method Calls **Step Over** allows one statement to execute, and if that one statement is a method call, the entire method will execute, leaving the current statement indicator at the statement *after* the method call. In other words, you will not see the current statement indicator move through the statements that are inside the method called.

Step Into Method Calls **Step Into** also allows one statement to execute, but if the statement is a method call, the current statement indicator will actually enter that method. Using **Step Into**, you can enter a method that has been called and then execute that method's statements one at a time if you choose.

Note that if you **Step Into** a standard method such as `System.out.println()`, you may see the actual Java source code for `println()`, if it is available, or a dialog box may pop up and ask you what to do about the situation. Most of the time, it is preferable to **Step Over** standard methods rather than to enter them, since it is usually safe to assume that their code is correct.

Step Out of a Method   **Step Out** causes the current statement indicator to exit from a method that you are currently inside. The method will finish executing, and then you will see the current statement indicator move to the statement in the caller, just after the call to the method you have exited.

In Sun ONE Studio, the **Step** commands provided are **Step Over, Step Into**, and **Step Out** and are found in the debugger's **Debug** menu.

Each of the debugging commands can also be executed via the keyboard or by clicking on the appropriate icon in the Debug Toolbar, which appears when you start debugging your program. Use whichever method suits you the best. Figure 4.2 shows the Sun ONE Studio **Debug** menu, with the **Debug** Toolbar on its right. Keyboard shortcuts are shown in the **Debug** menu, to the right of each command. Most Debug commands can be used only if the Source Editor window is selected.

As you execute your code with the debugger, keep in mind that your primary focus should be on examining the values of critical variables and observing the program's flow of control. The overall goal, of course, is to discover points in the program where errors occur.

4.3.3   A Note on Infinite Loops

If your program contains an infinite loop, you can easily detect it with **Step** commands. As you step through the code, at some point you will see the program get "stuck" inside some loop. In this situation, the current statement arrow will just keep going through the same code over, and over, and over, and over.... Use a **Finish** command to completely halt the Java program's execution.

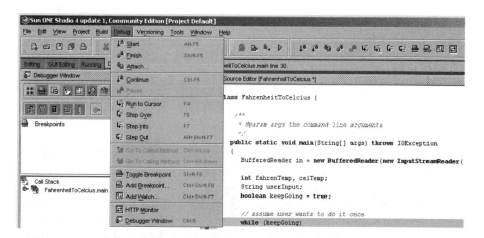

FIGURE 4.2

Debug menu in Sun ONE Studio.

4.3.4   Using Breakpoints

Sometimes, even stepping with **Step Over** method calls will be too slow. You may want to run your program at normal speed up to a certain point and then stop it to check the values of critical variables at that point. *Breakpoints* are specific statements at which you want execution to be suspended. They work like the cursor position in **Run to Cursor**. However, you can have only one cursor position, but you can have as many breakpoints as you want.

To insert a breakpoint in your code, you typically click either on the statement at which you want execution to stop or on some indicator next to that statement. For example, in Sun ONE Studio, click on the gray line beside a statement. A *red* square will appear in the gray line, indicating that the breakpoint is *set*. When you next run the program under the debugger's control, execution will automatically halt at this breakpoint.

You may insert as many breakpoints as you like, but if you put one in front of a nonexecutable Java statement, such as a comment, a declaration, or the like, the breakpoint will not work correctly, because a comment or declaration does not translate to a statement at which execution can stop. In Sun ONE Studio, not only can you set breakpoints on lines, as we have described, but you also can set them on method names, exceptions, classes, threads, and variables.

To remove a breakpoint in Sun ONE Studio, click on the red square so that it becomes a flat, gray line again. To remove all breakpoints simultaneously, right click on the Breakpoints root item in the **Breakpoints** Window in the **Debugger Window** and choose **Disable All** from the drop-down menu that appears.

You can control your breakpoints either by using the mouse, as we have described, or by using the **Debug** menu, the icons in the **Debug Toolbar**, the keyboard, or the drop-down menu. Again, choose the method that works best for you.

To run a program at normal speed until a breakpoint is encountered, choose **Start** or **Continue** from the Sun ONE Studio's **Debug** menu. Once the program has been interrupted by a breakpoint, you can resume execution or debug, using any of the commands already described. The **Step** commands may prove particularly useful once you have suspended execution at a breakpoint.

4.3.5   Watches

The **Variables** window lets you see the value of the variables that are in scope when the program is paused. Scope is the region of a program where a variable can be accessed. Sometimes, the value of an *expression* also is important for debugging. Using a watch, you can observe not just variable values, but also expression values. In Sun ONE Studio, you add an expression to the **Watches** window by selecting the expression in the Source Editor and then right clicking on it. When the expression is in scope and the program is paused, you will be able to see the value of the expression in the **Watches** window. You can also select variables to watch if you don't want to have the **Variables** window open and displaying all of the variables. You can add Watches by selecting the expression or variable to watch and then using the **Debug** menu or the **Debug** toolbar to add it to the **Watches** window.

4.3.6   Changing the Value of a Variable "On the Fly"

You can answer questions such as "Well, what if the variable X had the correct value of 2.3, instead of this wrong value that it seems to have?" by actually altering the value of the variable during the run, using the debugger. In Sun ONE Studio, click on the variable you want to change in the **Variables** pane in the **Debugger Window**. Wait a second for the cursor to change to an I-beam, and then just type in the new value you want to use. When you resume execution, the variable will have the value you just typed in.

4.3.7   Viewing Data Types

Data types (such as *int, double*, etc.) are usually not displayed alongside the names of variables in your debugger's windows; however, most debuggers allow you to indicate that you would like to see data types. In Sun ONE Studio, to tell the debugger to show you the data types that correspond to displayed variables, choose **Show Types** from the **Data** menu.

4.3.8   Displaying Values in an Object

The values of objects such as arrays and instances of classes are typically not all displayed in the debugger's window, unless you specifically choose to have them displayed. In Sun ONE Studio, to see all of the values in an object, you must click on the turner control symbol to the left of the variable name. You will then see the values displayed below the name.

Note that, as a default, many debuggers display only the memory address of the first element in a structured variable. This address can provide useful debugging information, depending on what your program needs to do. Because Java doesn't give you access to the memory addresses of objects, Sun ONE Studio provides a unique id number for each object so that you can tell whether two variables refer to the same object or to different objects.

4.3.9   Compiler and Debugger Preferences

Most compilers allow you to alter preferences that significantly affect the behavior of the debugger. Look for a **Preferences** or **Options** menu item to find out what debugging options you have available in your local system.

For example, Sun ONE Studio allows you to select the colors of breakpoints, disabled breakpoints, the current statement indicator, etc.

4.4 EXAMPLE: DEBUGGING A SAMPLE JAVA PROGRAM WITH SUN ONE STUDIO

In this section, we will look at a short, buggy Java program. Using the interactive debugger provided in Sun ONE Studio as an example, we will trace through the steps a programmer would go through in order to discover what is wrong in the program and then to fix it appropriately. The figures we present to illustrate the state of the debugger at various points were produced by Sun ONE Studio and are in fact "screen shots" of its debugging windows. Other modern IDEs provide similar features.

The Java program we will consider is intended to repeatedly read in Fahrenheit temperatures from the user and convert each to its equivalent Celsius value. After each temperature is converted, the user is asked whether he or she would like to convert another temperature. The process is supposed to repeat until the user indicates that he or she does not want to enter any more temperature values.

4.4.1 Sample Java Program: Buggy Version

Consider the following initial version of the program, which produces no syntax errors or warnings:

```java
import java.io.*;
public class FahrenheitToCelcius
{
    public static void main (String[] args)throws IOException
    {
        BufferedReader in = new BufferedReader(
            new InputStreamReader(System.in));
        int fahrenTemp, celTemp;
        String userInput;
        boolean keepGoing = true;
        // assume user wants to do it once
        while (keepGoing)
        {
            System.out.print("Enter a Fahrenheit temperature -> ");
            // get a temp and convert it
            userInput = in.readLine();
            fahrenTemp = Integer.parseInt(userInput);
            celTemp = (int)(5/9 * (fahrenTemp - 32));
            System.out.println("In Celsius that is " + celTemp);
            // ask if user wants to convert another
            System.out.println();
            System.out.println(
                    "Do you want to enter another temperature?");
```

```
            System.out.print(" Enter y or n -> ");
            userInput = in.readLine();
            // input error checking
            while (!userInput.equals("y") || !userInput.equals("n"))
            {
                System.out.print("Please enter y or n -> ");
                            userInput = in.readLine();
            }
            // reset flag
            keepGoing = userInput.equals("y");
        }
        System.exit(0);
    } // end of main
} // end of class FahrenheitToCelcius
```

When we run this program, it greatly taxes our patience and faith in computers, as we observe the following output dialogue:

```
Enter a Fahrenheit temperature -> 75
In Celsius that is 0
Do you want to enter another temperature?
 Enter y or n -> y
Please enter y or n -> y
Please enter y or n -> y
Please enter y or n -> y
Please enter y or n -> n
Please enter y or n ->
```

We finally have to forcibly quit the program (in Sun ONE Studio, right click on the class name in the **Execution** window and select **Terminate Process** from the drop-down menu) in order to end the misery. We then decide to use the interactive debugger to help us figure out what is wrong. The next few sections illustrate this process.

4.4.2   Sample Java Program: Using *Step* to Find the First Error

The first thing we see in the output of the preceding program is that the calculation of the Celsius temperature produces an incorrect value of 0 for a Fahrenheit value of 75. There are two critical variables here: fahrenTemp and celTemp. It is possible that fahrenTemp is somehow not being input and stored correctly. Alternatively, celTemp may not be calculated correctly. Let's check both possibilities by using the debugger to step through the program, one statement at a time, up to the point just before celTemp's value is output.

Figure 4.3 shows the Sun ONE Studio debugger's program window just at the point where we initiate execution of the program by clicking on the **Step**

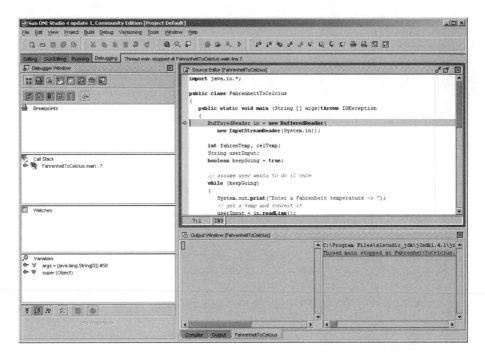

FIGURE 4.3

Debugging window at initial state.

Into icon on the **Debug** toolbar. In the windowpane labeled Call Stack, we see the stack trace. Method `main` in class `FahrenheitToCelcius` is the only active method we are concerned with here. In the pane labeled **Variables**, we see the `parameter args`. The four variables we have declared—`celTemp`, `fahrenTemp`, `keepGoing`, and `userInput`—have not been given values yet and so are not displayed. In the pane labeled Source Editor, we see our Java source program, with the current statement indicator shown as an arrow, pointing at the next statement to be executed.

We now use the **Step Over** command to execute the next few lines, bringing us to the state depicted in Figure 4.4, which shows the current statement indicator at the output statement for `celTemp`. This means that we have already entered a value for `fahrenTemp` (75) and can check the **Variables** pane to see whether that value is correct. It is correct, so `fahrenTemp` is not the problem. We next look at `celTemp`. It is 0, which we know is wrong. So we conclude that the assignment statement that calculates `celTemp` contains one or more errors.

Looking at the assignment, we notice that the formula looks superficially correct; however, we suspect that something must be wrong. Using watches, we can check the values of the subexpressions in the `celTemp` calculation by selecting each subexpression, right clicking, and then choosing **Add Watch** from

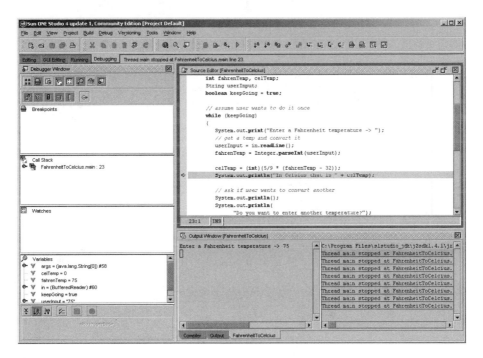

FIGURE 4.4

Debugging window at output line for celTemp, before correction.

the drop-down menu. Figure 4.5 shows the values of the subexpressions in the **Watches** window.

We see that the value of the expression "5/9" is zero! Because we are dividing two integer values, any fractional portion of the result is simply truncated.

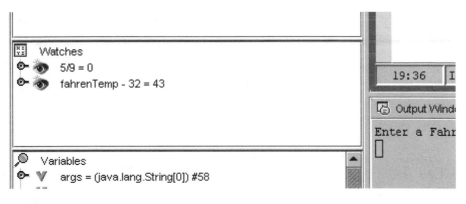

FIGURE 4.5

Watches window with the celTemp calculation subexpressions.

That makes the value of the entire calculation zero. If, instead, we evaluate "5/9" using real-number division, we can fix this one problem and see whether we then get a correct result.

Using the **Finish** command, we stop execution of the program, go back into our code, and change the assignment statement so that it reads "5.0/9.0" rather than "5/9". Then we start running the program again with **Step Into** and use **Step Over** to get to the same location.

Figure 4.6 shows that we have solved our first problem! The value of `celTemp` is now 23, which is correct. We decide to **Finish** the program run and celebrate our first small victory. Of course, the program must be tested with other temperature values before we can assume that it is running correctly for all possible values.

FIGURE 4.6

Debugging window at output line for `celTemp`, after correction.

4.4.3 Sample Java Program: Using Breakpoints to Find the Second Error

From our original program output, we can guess that we are stuck in an *infinite loop*: the loop in which we enter a "y" or an "n" to indicate whether we want to enter another temperature. There is one critical variable here: *userInput*.

We will set breakpoints at positions that are likely to help us determine exactly what the problem is with this loop. There are two possible reasons the loop might be infinite: (1) `response` is not read and stored correctly; (2) the logical expression at the loop entrance is faulty, so that even if `response` is read and stored correctly, we remain stuck.

Figure 4.7 shows the Sun ONE Studio debugger's program window just at the point where we have initiated execution of the program and chosen two breakpoints. To create a breakpoint with Sun ONE Studio, we click on the flattened line next to a Java statement. The line then turns into a red square, indicating that a breakpoint has been set. Remember that execution will stop just before the breakpoint statement executes.

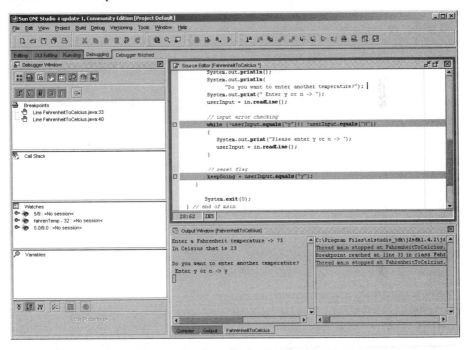

FIGURE 4.7

Debugging window after choosing two breakpoints.

Using **Start**, we now start the program, and it pauses when it hits the first breakpoint, at the top of the while loop we are concerned about. Figure 4.8 shows the state of the program when we have encountered this breakpoint and then used **Step Over** to find out what happens next. Assume that we entered a "y" when asked for a response.

Looking at the **Variables** window, we see that `response` is actually "y", which is correct here. This means that `response` is being read and stored correctly.

The critical variable, then, is fine, and the body of the loop should not execute at all. However, the current statement indicator shows that the next

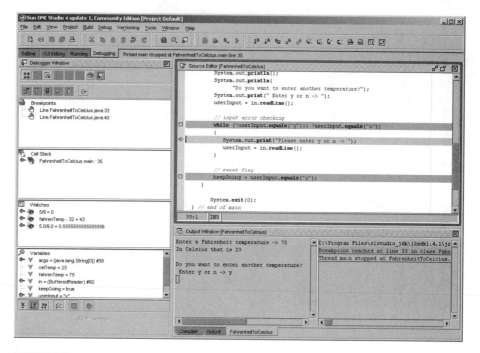

FIGURE 4.8

Debugging window after first breakpoint.

statement to be executed is the `System.out.println()` inside the loop that prints a prompt for a new value. Note that if we had correctly entered an "n", the exact same thing would have happened. We are indeed stuck in this loop! No matter what value we type in, we remain in the loop. We can change the value of `response` "on the fly" (described earlier) to whatever value we want in order to check that this is the case. We note that if we tried repeatedly entering values for `response`, we would see that the current statement indicator would never reach the second breakpoint that we set. The flow of control just can't get there.

Now what? The only possibility left is that the logical expression controlling the loop is wrong. Again, using watches, we can check the values of the subexpressions. Figure 4.9 shows the **Watches** window with the old watches replaced with new ones for the logical subexpressions in the while loop. We observe that the expression

```
!userInput.equals("y") || !userInput.equals("n")
```

is always true, regardless of the value of `response`. That is why the program can never exit the loop. Realizing this, we can **Finish** the program, change the expression to the correct version,

```
(!userInput.equals("y") && !userInput.equals("n"))
```

and run the program again. After this change, the program works correctly!

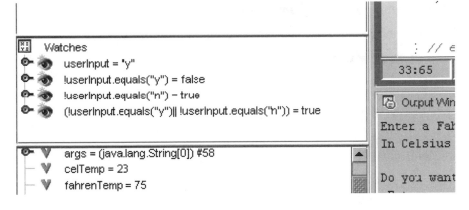

FIGURE 4.9

Watches window with while loop test information.

Figure 4.10 shows that once the logical expression has been corrected, the flow of control does indeed proceed to the second breakpoint we set, where the variable `keepGoing` is assigned a value. We can now stop at this point and verify that `keepGoing` is being set correctly if we wish. The infinite loop has been exited, and we have successfully corrected the program.

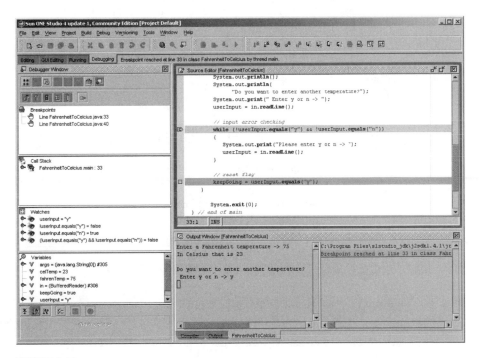

FIGURE 4.10

Debugging window at second breakpoint.

4.4.4 Sample Java Program: Corrected Version

The following code is the corrected program in its entirety:

```java
import java.io.*;
public class FahrenheitToCelcius
{
    public static void main (String[] args) throws IOException
    {
        BufferedReader in = new BufferedReader(
            new InputStreamReader(System.in));
        int fahrenTemp, celTemp;
        String userInput;
        boolean keepGoing = true;
        // assume user wants to do it once
        while (keepGoing)
        {
            System.out.print("Enter a Fahrenheit temperature -> ");
            // get a temp and convert it
            userInput = in.readLine();
            fahrenTemp = Integer.parseInt(userInput);
            celTemp = (int)(5.0/9.0 * (fahrenTemp - 32));
            System.out.println("In Celsius that is " + celTemp);
            // ask if user wants to convert another
            System.out.println();
            System.out.println(
                    "Do you want to enter another temperature?");
            System.out.print(" Enter y or n -> ");
            userInput = in.readLine();
            // input error checking
            while (!userInput.equals("y") && !userInput.equals("n"))
            {
                System.out.print("Please enter y or n -> ");
                userInput = in.readLine();
            }
            // reset flag
            keepGoing = userInput.equals("y");
        }
        System.exit(0);
    } // end of main
} // end of class FahrenheitToCelcius
```

When we run this version of the program, correct output is displayed as follows:

```
Enter a Fahrenheit temperature -> 75
In Celsius that is 23
Do you want to enter another temperature?
 Enter y or n -> y
Enter a Fahrenheit temperature -> 212
In Celsius that is 100
Do you want to enter another temperature?
 Enter y or n -> n
```

4.5   DEBUGGING WITH OTHER IDEs

Other integrated development environments (IDE) offer basically the same functionality that Sun ONE Studio provides, but in a slightly different format. To get you started with other IDEs, this section presents information about Borland JBuilder 5 Professional and Microsoft Visual J++ 6.0. Even if you have a different version of these IDEs, or a different IDE altogether, examining this section will give you some idea of where to look for debugging tools and how to invoke them.

We assume that you have studied Sections 4.3 and 4.4. Most of the information presented in the current section is in the form of tables that have data for Sun ONE Studio as well as JBuilder and Visual J++. If you aren't sure what a row in a table means, look in the previous sections for the explanation of what it means in Sun ONE Studio.

4.5.1   Using Borland JBuilder 5 Professional

To debug a program in Borland JBuilder, make a new project and add your files to it. For an application, you must set the main class by choosing **Project Properties** from the **Project** menu, then clicking on the **Run** tab, and, finally, choosing the class that contains the declaration of main. Now you can run or debug your program by choosing the corresponding item from the **Run** menu.

The Borland JBuilder graphical user interface displays the Java program in the large window and, if the program is running, includes an arrow that points to the next statement to be executed. Figure 4.11 illustrates Borland JBuilder's user interface.

If you choose **Debug Project** from the **Run** menu, the debugger window appears at the bottom and lets you choose what program information you want to see. Available debug information includes the variables, the call stack, your breakpoints, and your watches. You can also monitor multiple debug sessions and multiple threads or explore any of the classes used in your program.

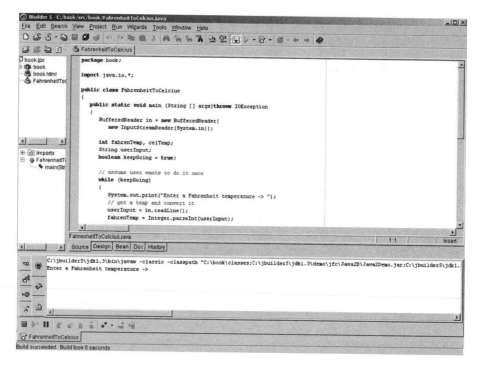

FIGURE 4.11

Borland JBuilder's graphical user interface in debug mode.

In Borland JBuilder, you select which types of information to monitor by clicking on the tabs on the side of the debugger window. One of these tabs displays an output window that lets you see the output of your program as it executes and lets you type in any required input. The debug window tabs and toolbar have "tooltips" to let you know what they do. Tooltips are tiny popup windows with explanatory text that appear when your cursor stays on a control GUI. (See Figure 4.12.)

FIGURE 4.12

Debug window tabs and toolbar.

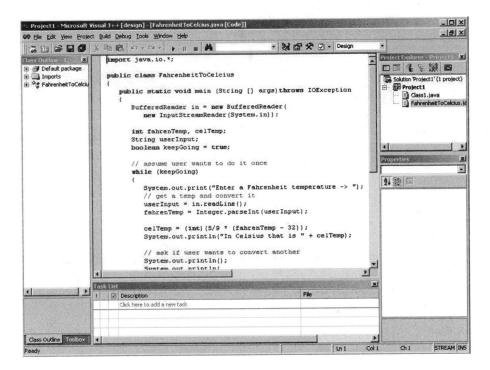

FIGURE 4.13

The Microsoft Visual J++ graphical user interface.

4.5.2   Using Microsoft Visual J++ 6.0

To debug a program in Microsoft Visual J++, make a new project and type your code in it. Now you can run your program, with or without debugging, by choosing the corresponding item from the **Debug** menu.

The Microsoft Visual J++ graphical user interface displays the Java program in the large window in the center, and if the program is running, includes an arrow that points to the next statement to be executed. Figure 4.13 shows an example of the user interface.

By default, no debugging windows are displayed. You choose which ones you want to see by going to the **View** menu and selecting **Debug Windows.** A list of debug windows is then displayed. Available debug information includes the variables, the call stack, your threads, and your watches. If you want to see the debug toolbar, go to the **View** menu, choose **Toolbars**, and then select **Debug.** The debug toolbar will appear below the menu bar. Figure 4.14 shows the Visual J++ user interface with the debug toolbar showing and the list of available debug windows.

4.5.3   Main Debugging Menu

Most interactive debuggers have a menu containing the majority of the commonly used debugging commands. The name of the menu and the

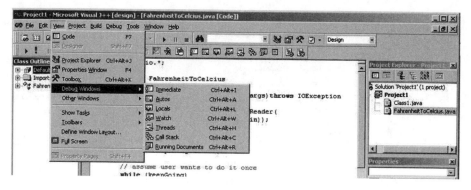

FIGURE 4.14

The Microsoft Visual J++ graphical user interface with the debug toolbar.

names of the commands vary slightly. Table 4.1 gives the name of the main debugging menu and some of the command names in the menu for each of the three IDEs. Equivalent commands, when they exist, are shown in the same row of the table.

TABLE 4.1 Comparison of Main Debugging Menu Commands

Sun ONE Studio **Debug** menu	Borland JBuilder **Run** menu	Microsoft Visual J++ **Debug** menu
Start	Debug Project	Start
Finish	Reset Program	End
Pause	Pause Program	Break
Continue	Resume Program	Continue
Run to Cursor	Run to Cursor	Run to Cursor
	Run to End of Method	
Step Into	Step Into	Step Into
Step Over	Step Over	Step Over
Step Out	Step Out	Step Out
Add Watch	Add Watch	
Add Breakpoint	Add Breakpoint	
Toggle Breakpoint		
		Remove Breakpoint
		Disable Breakpoint
	View Breakpoints	Breakpoints

Some debugging commands can be executed by using keyboard shortcuts. Figure 4.15 shows the Borland JBuilder Run menu and Figure 4.16 shows the Microsoft Visual J++ Debug menu. Keyboard shortcuts are shown in the Run menu to the right of each command. Commands with icons on the left can also be executed from the debugging toolbar at the bottom of the window.

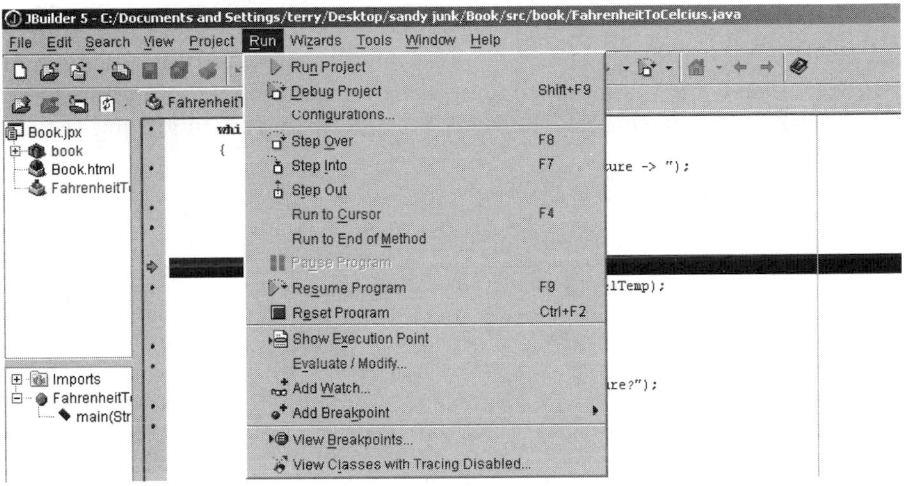

FIGURE 4.15

Run menu with debug commands in Borland JBuilder.

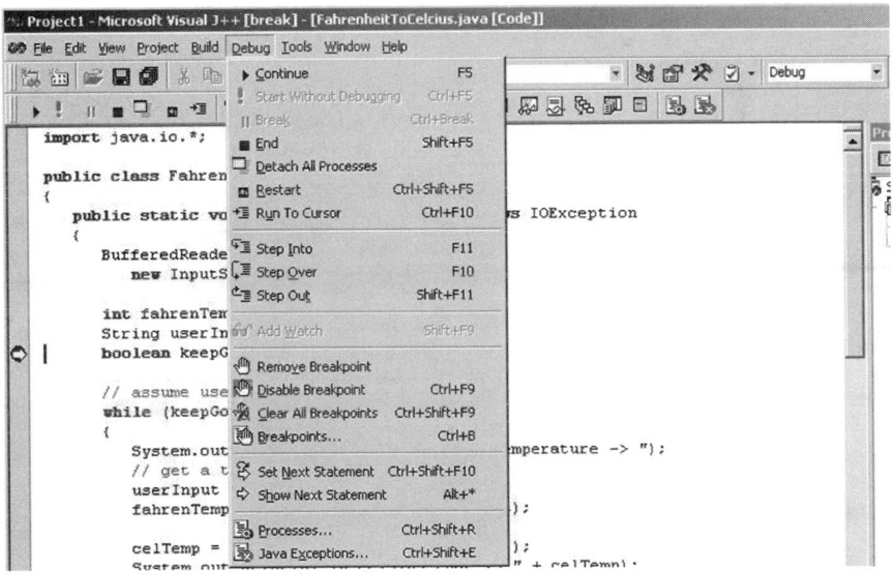

Figure 4.16

Debug menu with debug commands in Microsoft Visual J++.

4.5.4 Breakpoints

To insert a breakpoint in your code, you typically click on the statement at which you want execution to stop or on some indicator next to that statement. (See Table 4.2.) Clicking on the same location a second time removes the breakpoint.

TABLE 4.2 Comparison of Breakpoint Commands

	Sun ONE Studio	Borland JBuilder	Microsoft Visual J++
Where to click	Gray line beside the statement	Tiny blue diamond beside the statement	Gray line beside the statement
Breakpoint icon	Red square	Red circle	Very dark red circle
Disable all	Right click on the breakpoint's root item in the Debugger Window, and choose **Disable All** from the drop-down menu	Choose **View Breakpoints** from the **Run** menu, right click on the dialog box that appears, and choose **Remove All** from the drop-down menu	Choose **Clear All Breakpoints** from the **Debug** menu
Other breakpoint locations	Method names, exceptions, classes, threads, variables	Method names, exceptions, classes	Method names

4.5.5 Watches

The **Variables** window lets you see the value of the variables that are in scope when the program is paused. (See Table 4.3.) **Watches** let you see the values of variables, expressions in the code, or arbitrary expressions. As long as the variables in an expression are in scope, you can see their current values or the values of any expressions that use those variables.

TABLE 4.3 Comparison of Variables and Watches Commands

	Sun ONE Studio	Borland JBuilder	Microsoft Visual J++
Variables in scope	Variables window	Data watches window	Autos window and Locals window
Expressions	Select expression in the source code and right click it In **Debug** menu choose **Add Watch**	Select expression in the source code and right click it In **Run** menu choose **Add Watch**	Select expression in the source code and right click it In **Debug** menu choose **Add Watch**

4.5.6   Changing the Value of a Variable "On the Fly"

You can answer questions such as "Well, what if the variable X did have the correct value of 2.3 instead of this wrong value it seems to have?" by actually altering the value of the variable during the run, using the debugger. (See Table 4.4.)

TABLE 4.4   Comparison of How to Change Variables "On the Fly"

Sun ONE Studio	Borland JBuilder	Microsoft Visual J++
Click on the variable you want to change in the Variables window. Wait for the cursor to change to an I beam, and then type in the new value.	Right click on the variable you want to change in the variables section of the **Threads, call stacks and data** tab in the debug window.	Click on the value you want to change in either the Autos window or the Locals window.

4.5.7   Compiler and Debugger Preferences

Most compilers allow you to alter the preferences of the debugger. (See Table 4.5.) Doing so, however, significantly affects the behavior of the debugger.

TABLE 4.5   Comparison of Alter Preferences Commands

Sun ONE Studio	Borland JBuilder	Microsoft Visual J++
In **Tools** menu, choose **Editor Options** In **Tools** menu, choose **IDE Options**	In **Tools** menu, choose **Editor Options** In **Tools** menu, choose **IDE Options**	In **Tools** menu, choose **Options** In **Tools** menu, choose **Options**

APPENDIX A

Checklist of Common Bugs in First Programs

In this appendix, we summarize some of the most common bugs found in students' first programs, based on our experience with introductory programming classes over the past decade. The checklist that follows is by no means exhaustive, but is given to help beginning programmers analyze their code in advance for potential bugs. More details about how to detect and correct these bugs (errors) are given in the sections of the book shown in parentheses:

1. Array index out of bounds (Sec. 2.4.2)
2. Bad input data not recognized (Sec. 3.2.1)
3. Black not used when required (Sec. 2.5.2)
4. Calling a method with wrong arguments (Sec. 2.2.2)
5. Code inside a loop that does not belong there (Sec. 2.5.2)
6. Dangling `else` (Sec. 2.5.2)
7. Division by zero (Sec. 1.3)
8. `If` condition not used properly (Secs. 2.5.2, 3.2.3)
9. Infinite loop (Secs. 2.5.2, 4.3.3)
10. Left-hand side of assignment does not contain a variable (Sec. 2.2.2)
11. Lines of code put outside of methods (Sec. 2.2.2)
12. Local variable not initialized (Sec. 2.2.2)
13. Missing semicolon in simple statements (Sec. 2.2.2)
14. Operator precedence misunderstood (Sec. 2.5.2)
15. Off-by-one error in a loop (Sec. 2.5.2)

16. Strings not terminated (Sec. 2.2.2)
17. Switch statement error (Sec. 3.2.2)
18. Undeclared variable name (Sec. 2.2.2)
19. Undefined class name (Sec. 2.2.2)
20. Unmatched parentheses (Sec. 2.2.2)
21. Value-returning method has no return statement (Sec. 2.2.2)
22. Using "=" when "==" is intended (Secs. 2.2.2, 2.5.2)
23. Using objects that are null (Sec. 2.4.2)
24. While loop error (Sec. 2.5.2)

APPENDIX B

Checklist for Error Detection and Prevention

The details of error detection and prevention are well covered by outstanding programmers and authors, such as Brian Kernighan and Rob Pike in their book *The Practice of Programming*. Our intent here is to categorize the fundamental ideas expressed by these and other experienced programmers as a checklist for the new programmer and, hopefully, lead you to read those works in depth as you progress in your programming skills.

B.1 ERROR DETECTION METHODS

Error detection methods are used to find errors that have caused a program to run incorrectly. Syntax errors will automatically be detected by your Java compiler. Semantic errors include those errors which cause the program to crash or to go into an infinite loop. Other semantic errors may not cause any obvious crashes or loops, but result in incorrect output. Both types of semantic errors can usually be detected with the following methods:

1. Use the tracing method described in this book (see Chapter 3) to display the values of critical variables, including arrays, strings, and simple variables. Display the values both before and after their modification in the program. The more tracing statements you put into the program, the more you can localize the problem and target the real error.

2. Get a trace of method calls to see whether methods are being called in the correct sequence. This feature is usually provided as part of an interactive debugger. (See Chapter 4.) The debugger is an effective

tool for error detection, especially when simple print tracing fails to find the error.

3. Once an error is found, correct it immediately while you understand what the problem is and can easily make the fix. Then check to see whether the same mistake has been made elsewhere, and fix those occurrences immediately.

4. Examine the most recent changes to the program's code. Often, corrections to old errors contain new errors, so it is useful to carefully check all changes just made.

5. Some irreproducible errors may be due to undefined behavior in the programming language. For example, n = n++ + ++n; produces different behavior on different compilers. Try to make the error reproducible. Being able to easily reproduce its occurrence while making small changes in your code will help in locating the problem. Errors that are not reproducible are probably due to system or hardware errors and may not be in your code.

B.2   ERROR PREVENTION AND TESTING METHODS

1. Use good design techniques, good programming style (use consistent indentation, avoid global variables, etc.), and well-designed interfaces among functions and with the user.

2. Study your code thoroughly after typing it in and before running it. This activity is often referred to as a *code inspection* or *walk-through*. Explain your code to someone else if possible—ideally, to another programmer—as part of the walk-through.

3. Make your program self-documenting, with comments that describe the definitions of all variables; the purpose of, and interfaces to, methods; and a brief description of the purpose of each control structure (e.g., a loop or a selection statement).

4. Insert self-checking code to test for the possibility of bad input data to the program, and protect the program from crashing when bad data is read. This activity is also referred to as *defensive programming*.

5. Test your code at the boundary values for variables and for pre- and postconditions. Testing in this manner involves placing trace variables just before and after control structures (selection statements such as if and switch; looping statements such as while, do, and for; and method calls) are entered; tracing values used inside these control structures, including testing the execution of each branch in selection statements; and testing for, while, and do loops so that their indexes are properly set before the loop executes and when it finishes. This technique can also be used to avoid the division-by-zero problem.

6. Avoid the error recurrence problem by keeping a log of all bugs fixed.

7. Test your program incrementally, after each method is written, or subdivide a method into parts that can be tested independently. Use stub and driver methods to test individual methods in your program. Don't wait until you have *all* the code written before doing any testing. By then, the errors will be much harder to localize and detect.

8. Write down the preconditions and postconditions for each method. For example, for a particular method, what must be true when the method is called? What must be true when the program exits the method? Then use print tracing, a debugger, or assertions to check your conditions.

9. Consider these behavioral properties in all programs:

    - *correctness*. Does the program produce correct output if it is given correct input?

    - *reliability* (robustness). Does the program handle incorrect data properly?

    - *utility*. Is the program easy to use?

    - *performance*. Is the program efficient? That is, does it execute quickly enough to satisfy the needs of the user of the program?

B.3   WHERE TO INSERT TRACES AND WHAT VARIABLES TO DISPLAY

In this section, we offer some rules of thumb about where to insert traces into your Java program code and what variables to display for each type of trace. Think of these rules as constituting a checklist that can be added to or subtracted from, depending on the specific conditions in your program code.

Note that the following techniques can also be employed effectively when using an interactive debugger to determine where breakpoints should be placed and what critical variables should be attended to:

1. Sequential code (no control statements)
    - Display critical variables at the beginning and the end of each 10 to 15 lines of purely sequential code.

2. If statements
    - Display critical variables just before and after `if` and `else` conditions.

3. `While` and `for` loops
    - Display critical variables just before and after `while` and `for` blocks.
    - Display critical variables within `while` or `for` loops consistently, just before or after an increment or decrement of a loop counter.
    - Display the loop counter.

4. Methods
   - Display all parameters before and after each method entry.
   - Display all parameters and return values before and after each method exit.
5. Arrays
   - Display array components and array index values before and after array contents have been modified.
6. Character strings
   - Display critical variables before and after each use of a string method.

Bibliography

Deitel, H.M. and Deitel, P.J. *Java: How to Program*, 5th ed., Prentice Hall, 2003.

Ford, A.R. and Teorey, T.J. *Practical Debugging in* C++, Prentice Hall, 2002.

Haggar, P. *Practical Java*, Addison-Wesley, 2000.

Kernighan, B.W. and Pike, R. *The Practice of Programming*, Addison-Wesley, 1999.

Lencevicius, R. *Advanced Debugging Methods*, Kluwer Academic Publishing, 2000.

Mitchell, W.D. *Debugging Java: Troubleshooting for Programs*, McGraw-Hill, 2000.

Robbins, J. *Debugging Applications*, Microsoft Press, 2000.

Rosenberg, J.B. *How Debuggers Work: Algorithms, Data Structures, and Architecture*, Wiley, 1996.

Stitt, M. *Debugging: Creative Techniques and Tools for Software Repair*, Wiley, 1992.

Telles, M.A., Hsieh, Y., and Telles, M. *The Science of Debugging*, The Coriolis Group, 2001.

Vermeulen, A. (Ed.) *The Elements of Java Style*, Cambridge University Press, 2000.

Index

About the Authors

Sandra L. Bartlett is an Adjunct Assistant Professor of Electrical Engineering and Computer Science in the School of Information at the University of Michigan. She has taught numerous introductory courses in Java and has developed a variety of debugging practices that she promotes in her classes. She received a Ph.D. from the University of Michigan.

Gary S. Tyson is an Assistant Professor of Electrical Engineering and Computer Science at the University of Michigan. He received his Ph.D. in Computer Science at the University of California at Davis. His current interests are in compilers and programming languages, as well as computer architecture and computer optimization.

Ann R. Ford is currently a Lecturer of Electrical Engineering and Computer Science at the University of Michigan. She has taught introductory courses in programming for the past 10 years and has applied and refined debugging principles for many students. She received a B.A. degree in Psychology from SUNY at Buffalo and an M.S. degree in computer and communication science from the University of Michigan.

Toby J. Teorey is a Professor of Electrical Engineering and Computer Science at the University of Michigan. He received a B.S. and M.S. degrees in Electrical Engineering from the University of Arizona and a Ph.D. in Computer Science from the University of Wisconsin. He is the author of *Database Modeling and Design* (1999) and coauthor (with Ann Ford) of *Practical Debugging in C++* (2002). He has taught extensively in both introductory and advanced programming classes.

Students are encouraged to have an active involvement in their own learning, through tutorials and research projects.

NOTTINGHAM UNIVERSITY

University of Nottingham, University Park, Nottingham NG7 2RD
Tel: 0115 951 5151

The School of Psychology is one of the largest and strongest in the country with excellent laboratories and IT facilities. There are leading research groups in developmental psychology, cognition and cognitive neuroscience and in computational modelling. The first and second years contain all the compulsory core modules for BPS recognition, enabling finalists to concentrate on areas of interest. Practical and statistical modules are taken in the first two years to prepare for the third year project which accounts for one third of the final-year grade. All students register for a BSc degree, although applicants with arts and humanities A-levels, or a mixture, are encouraged to apply. Students take different subsidiary modules in their first year depending on their background. There is a joint Honours programme with Philosophy and a BSc in Psychology and Cognitive Neuroscience.

OXFORD BROOKES UNIVERSITY

Oxford Brookes University, Gipsy Lane, Headington, Oxford OX3 0BP
Tel: 01865 484848

Within the School of Social Sciences and Law, Psychology is a three-year BA/BSc course studied either as a single Honours degree or as a joint degree with one from over 60 other subjects from across the University. It is possible to change to a single Honours course after the first year. The department recently received an 'excellent' quality assurance rating. The course is modular and emphasises practical and laboratory experience. A range of assessments is used including seminars, coursework and examinations. With an appropriate course of study, students obtain GBR. The department also offers a one-year conversion course to the GBR for non-psychology graduates.

OXFORD
UNIVERSITY

University of Oxford, Admissions Office, Wellington Square,
Oxford OX1 2JD
Tel: 01865 270000

You can study Psychology at Oxford in two ways: either as a part
subject in the joint Honours school with Philosophy and/or
Physiology, or as a subject on its own in Experimental Psychology.
Either route can qualify for BPS GBR. Decisions on selection are
made by individual colleges, not by the Department of
Experimental Psychology. You should choose a college which has a
tutor in Psychology (not available at Exeter, Keble, Lincoln,
Mansfield, Merton, St Peter's or Trinity). The first two terms
consist of three introductory courses. You will then be examined at
the end of your second term (an examination called Prelims) which
allows you to move on to Part 1 (core courses) and Part 2 (options)
of the Final Honours School.

PAISLEY
UNIVERSITY

University of Paisley, Paisley PA1 2BE
Tel: 0141 848 3000

The Psychology Sciences programme can be taken over three years
for a BA or four years for a BA Honours. The programme helps
students use the findings, theories and methods of psychology to
explore and understand life in contemporary society. In the final
year you can choose 'elective' modules from across the University,
in addition to the core elements of the programme. Paisley offers a
comprehensive personal tutorial system and provides courses
geared towards specific careers or postgraduate study. The degree is
recognised by the BPS as conferring GBR.

PLYMOUTH
UNIVERSITY

University of Plymouth, Drake Circus, Plymouth PL4 8AA
Tel: 01752 600600

There are opportunities to study psychology as a single or joint
degree and to obtain work experience under two different routes.
The first way is through the Visits Programme in which students
attend an organisation that does work relevant to psychology.
Attendance is for one half-day per week for one semester. This
programme is the first of its kind in the UK. The second route is

through a sandwich placement year. Successful completion of the year entitles you to the Certificate of Industrial and Professional Experience.

PORTSMOUTH UNIVERSITY

University of Portsmouth, Winston Churchill Avenue, Portsmouth PO1 2UP
Tel: 023 9284 6313

The Department of Psychology offers a single Honours BSc in Psychology, combined Honours BSc in Psychology with Criminology and several other Honours degrees with psychology as a minor. These degrees are delivered over three years with two semesters per year, but may also be taken on a part-time basis over six years. The Psychology BSc emphasises a 'hands-on' approach to the subject and encourages links with ongoing staff research. The department has well-equipped laboratory facilities and current research interests include: child witnesses; police interviewing; primate communication; colour perception; the detection of deception; ecological approaches to intentionality; social understanding and locomotion; psychophysiology and neuropsychology.

QUEEN MARGARET COLLEGE

Queen Margaret College, Clerwood Terrace, Edinburgh EH12 8TS
Tel: 0131 317 3000

Queen Margaret University College is situated in Edinburgh. Degrees are offered over three or four years; the three year option provides an Ordinary degree. Psychology can be studied at Honours level; either as a single Honours degree (BSc (Hons) Psychology), or specialising in Health Psychology (BSc (Hons) Health Psychology), over four years. It is also possible to include Psychology as part of the joint degrees scheme, either as a major, joint or minor subject, with eg Sociology and Social Policy, or Business and Marketing. Success at Honours level in any of these awards confers eligibility for Graduate Membership of the BPS and Graduate Basis for Registration. Health Psychology is a particular speciality at QMUC, although staff have a wide variety of interests.

READING UNIVERSITY	The University of Reading, Whiteknights, Reading RG6 6AH Tel: 0118 987 5123

The School of Psychology offers single Honours BSc degree programmes in Psychology, in Psychology, Childhood and Ageing, and in Psychology, Mental and Physical Health. Psychology may also be combined with Sociology, Linguistics, Philosophy, Art, Biology, Statistics or Mathematics. All these degree programmes meet the requirements for graduate membership of the BPS and for the Graduate Basis for Recognition (GBR) which is the first step towards becoming a Chartered Psychologist.

UNIVERSITY OF SURREY, ROEHAMPTON	Whitelands College, West Hill, London SW15 3SN Tel: 020 8392 3000

A BSc in Psychology and Counselling is offered here and was the first of its kind in Britain. You will learn basic counselling skills and participate in personal growth work as well as psychology. It has links with a number of hospitals, counselling centres and universities. There is a BSc single Honours Psychology programme as well as a BA/BSc combined degree programme.

ST ANDREWS UNIVERSITY	University of St Andrews, College Gate, St Andrews, Fife KY16 9Al Tel: 01334 476161

Psychology may be taken as a first year subject in either the Arts or Sciences. A more advanced course can be taken in the second year and students who do well in this can go on to take the two-year Honours Psychology degree course either as a single subject or jointly with one of a wide range of alternatives.

SHEFFIELD HALLAM UNIVERSITY	Sheffield Hallam University, Howard Street, Sheffield S1 1WB Tel: 0114 272 0911

Psychology is located in the School of Health and Community Studies under an Applied Social Studies Honours degree programme. One of the main features is its international focus; it has links with other European countries so studying overseas is an option.